BROKEN

*Returning in Desperation
to the Cross*

Matthias Ponce-de-Leon

WESTBOW
PRESS®
A DIVISION OF THOMAS NELSON
& ZONDERVAN

Scripture taken from the King James Version of the Bible.

Scripture taken from the Holy Bible, NEW INTERNATIONAL
VERSION®. Copyright © 1973, 1978, 1984 by Biblica, Inc. All rights
reserved worldwide. Used by permission. NEW INTERNATIONAL
VERSION® and NIV® are registered trademarks of Biblica,
Inc. Use of either trademark for the offering of goods or services
requires the prior written consent of Biblica US, Inc.

WestBow Press books may be ordered through
booksellers or by contacting:

WestBow Press
A Division of Thomas Nelson & Zondervan
1663 Liberty Drive
Bloomington, IN 47403
www.westbowpress.com
1 (866) 928-1240

Because of the dynamic nature of the Internet, any web addresses or
links contained in this book may have changed since publication and
may no longer be valid. The views expressed in this work are solely those
of the author and do not necessarily reflect the views of the publisher,
and the publisher hereby disclaims any responsibility for them.

Any people depicted in stock imagery provided by Thinkstock are
models, and such images are being used for illustrative purposes only.
Certain stock imagery © Thinkstock.

ISBN: 978-1-5127-2426-4 (sc)
ISBN: 978-1-5127-2427-1 (e)

Library of Congress Control Number: 2015920754

Print information available on the last page.

WestBow Press rev. date: 01/11/2016

Contents

For His Glory

Acknowledgements

My wife Alexis—Who has walked with me through every form of insanity from which I suffered and who nurses me in the "Jesus Asylum" today.

Aliece, Isaac and Peyton—For loving their crazy Dad.

Darold—Thank you for teaching me about forgiveness. Thank you for telling me about Jesus.

Pastor Jerry—For countless hours spent together in fellowship, the Word and prayer. The idea for this text was given by The Lord through our time together. For sharing your wisdom and for your guiding hand.

Pastor Lon and Kay—For your instruction, example of excellence and passion for people. For helping me to believe that this book was possible in more ways than you know.

Pastor Wess—For bring this stray cat in off the porch. For the milk and the meat you fed me.

Amy—For reminding me that this book needs to sound like me, and for helping to keep it that way.

The Saints of:

Arlington First Baptist Church, Oak Level Baptist Church, and Friendship Baptist Church—for their patience, love, partnership and support.

The many readers, editors, and listeners who spent time with this text in its various stages. Those who endured unending "Hey listen to this for a minute..." moments and who offered invaluable advice.

Foreword

Never in recent History has there been a greater need for revival than today. The church in America is in deep trouble. America itself is being lost to paganism as lostness rapidly increases. All the while, the church wastes away in sin, apathy, complacency and arrogance. The church often wants to place the blame for this moral and spiritual collapse on political parties, the economic downfall, racial tension, the lost world and even the devil himself. But in reality, the body of Christ in America must own up to the fact that it is responsible. We (believers) have departed from the Lord and He is judging us and this nation because of our sin. As James says—we have become friends of the world through our self-centeredness and self-reliance (prayerlessness)—making us God's enemy (see James 4:1-6). His call to His people in America is simple –"Be Ye Holy as I Am Holy (1 Peter 1:16).

Returning to the Lord in holiness can only begin one way—God's way! Second Chronicles 7:14 says,

"If my people who are called by My name will humble themselves, pray and seek My face, I will hear from heaven, forgive their sin and heal their land." Thus one must begin the journey toward revival through humility and brokenness before God. This is the place to start. To humble oneself before God is to do so in great abandonment to self—it begins with me—not someone else. It begins with total surrender as a believer sets his/her heart and life totally toward the Lord. He therefore is our only hope for survival. He is God!

In *Broken: Returning in Desperation to the Cross* Matty Ponce-de-Leon weaves together his story and the Gospel story with the biblical theme of brokenness. The reader is challenged to see the journey of brokenness not as a one-time event, but as a lifestyle that is a daily part of a believer's relationship with Christ. Through humble obedience to God's Word, brokenness over sin, prayer and service with and through the body of Christ, believers are challenged toward a daily walk that involves clean hands and pure hearts (see Psalm 24:3-4). The challenge is to take seriously the role that brokenness over sin and self requires daily dependence upon Jesus and His amazing grace, mercy and love through His finished work on the cross.

Broken is well worth the read and can be used by individuals, small groups and churches. I recommend it to you. I also commend Matty Ponce-de-Leon on a job well done. May the Lord use *Broken* to spur believers and churches toward revival—impacting lostness, for His Glory! Do it Lord Jesus!

J. Chris Schofield, Ph.D.
Wake Forest, NC

Preface

This book is written for those saints, seekers and students of the Word, who desire to live excellent for Christ. For those who understand that as long as we bear our robes of flesh, we will always be just "starting out" on our journey with the Lord. These thoughts are intended simply to be helpful as you take another step together with Him.

I have attempted not to be too technical or laborious with scriptural examples. As I am slightly nerdy in this regard, this has been an exercise in discipline for me. I have, however, written this with the student of the Word in mind. I love the Word, spend time in study daily and hold it in the highest regard. Indeed, much of this writing centers around the impact and influence of Truth upon our lives.

When Christ ministered during the span of His incarnation, He spoke often to those who identified themselves as God's people. In addressing them, He spoke with the assumption that they had a familiarity with the Word of God.[1] When Paul preached to the Jews, he referenced the Scripture in a manner that assumed the same familiarity.[2] The implication of these manners of ministry is clear: We cannot (and should not think that we can) live progressive and powerful lives as God's people apart from His Truth.[3]

So, I encourage you to be diligent in His Word and humble in your walk. Seek the manifestation of His Truth in your life with the desperation of the parched and starving people we are apart from Him. Drink deeply from the water of the Word.

Introduction

It's worth it: Everything we go through, every "labor of love," every heartache, every insult, every frustration, every sleepless night, every criticism, every false accusation, every disappointment, every dollar spent, every tear, every pain, every hard truth, every examination of oneself—it's worth it. The cross of Calvary tells us so. Jesus endured everything He shouldn't have[1] that we might know a power, peace and productivity that we couldn't have on our own. The transformation of our lives as believers and the change of our eternal destiny is an unbelievable miracle with magnificent implications. What a tragedy it is, therefore, when we waste it. When our walk is not *"circumspect,"*[2] and we miss the chance to live *"unto the measure of the stature of the fullness of Christ."*[3]

Let me begin by saying, it is not my desire to share a series of criticisms, rebukes or barbed accusations against the Church. It is the desire of my heart to share a series of burdens that I hope you, in turn, will share and bear with me. What is addressed in these pages comes not from the jaded heart of the jilted or the resentful heart of the rejected. It comes, as sincerely as I know how, from the broken heart of a brother.

Sometimes I truly count it a blessing to have not spent a lifetime being indoctrinated with so many of the crippling traditions amongst the body of Christ. This statement is not some declarative which attempts to render all traditions bad or useless. Many traditions promote unity and edify through warm memories and expressions of fellowship. Often, we find great comfort there. Many, while potentially an issue of poor stewardship, are stirring through their nostalgia and anticipatory excitement (treat bags anyone?)

There are, however, some traditional behaviors that are entirely unbiblical, yet I have found to be nearly universal among the assemblies of believers I have encountered. We have a tendency, at times, to treat one another so poorly, so insensitively, that it is amazing we keep re-assembling at all. At times, we are so apathetic ("I've pulled my time in service." "Why can't someone else do it?"), it is amazing we accomplish anything at all. Often (and sadly) the greatest accomplishments of the Church are things we have accomplished primarily for our personal benefits and enjoyments (Yes, I want a "Family Life Center" too). With this self-serving attitude, it becomes so easy for anyone who stands in the way of what we want to be labeled as "against God's will." Even worse, these self-centered desires are catalysts in our often poor view and treatment of those outside the Church as well, for they jeopardize the little "kingdoms" we create for ourselves. Instead of an assembly of the grateful redeemed we become a bunch of grouchy rejecters. I won't be the first person to note that the shift waiters and waitresses dislike working the most is Sunday lunch—where the demands are highest, the criticisms are loudest and the tips are the smallest. Nor will I be the first to say that there are lost, needy people in the shadows of our steeples.

I used to say often, "If everyone thinks I'm a jerk, I won't be able to tell anyone about Jesus." On the basis of this thought (both in evangelism and discipleship), I would make an effort toward outward appearances of compassion and care, smiles in the right directions and presence in the right places. While the response from those I encountered was often positive, my regard for those I encountered often was not. This insincere heart with which I have at times walked has brought about quick regressions into "tough-love" and "brutal-truth" tactics. Make no mistake, at times a shaking-up is necessary for all of our lives. But a steady diet of insensitive "straight shooting" is nothing close to the example set forth by our Lord. My hypocrisy has been convicting. In recent times I've taken to reminding myself in a more simple fashion, "if *I am a jerk*, I won't be able to tell anyone about Jesus." The unfortunate truth is that sometimes the reason we are viewed as hypocrites (this is also an entirely unoriginal thought) is because we actually are. Ouch.

Let me explain from where I think the stirring of these burdens is coming. The Body of Christ loved me when I was unlovable. The Body of Christ taught me when I was completely unknowledgeable. They fed me milk when I couldn't even hold the bottle for myself. I would not be sitting and standing where I am so privileged to be today were it not for the work of the Lord through the willingness of His Saints. This is why, knowing the great power and potential that rests within the Body of Christ, I am concerned by what I so often observe among the brethren. Why are we so comfortable with treating one another so poorly? Why are we so comfortable complaining, griping and criticizing? Why do we so readily settle into long-term resentment and unforgiveness toward one another? Do we not see that how we relate with each other will either make or break our witness to the world? Do we not see that self-centered apathy is one of the clearest violations against the Great Commission that there is?

I don't have a solution or some spiritual button to push to make these questions become moot, but I know the answer lies at the foot of the cross. Think back to that day. Think to the time when there was no other way, no other choice, no other hope but Jesus. Do you remember how desperate you were? You weren't just going along one day thinking, "Everything's so great, I think I'll call upon Jesus to rescue me," were you? Now ask yourself, "Am I *still* that desperate for Jesus? Am I still broken before Him?" Some may not characterize the moment of salvation as a desperate one. Scripture, however, illustrates a very severe and dramatic picture of the condition of the unregenerate.[4]

It is such a struggle for believers to maintain the desperation of that day. I know it has been for me. Some question if they even need to. ("Jesus saved me to make me strong right? To bless me, right? Isn't that why I came? I'm here for my blessing!" See Paul in 2 Corinthians 12:10 for further thoughts on this.) The struggle to maintain an abandon and faith that has the power to move mountains is, in part, manifested by our brazen behaviors toward one another. Lack of compassion, sharp tongues, and rudeness among the brethren is a product of the attitude of "Why should I have to behave otherwise?" Worse still, these types of behavior are so prevalent that it is a good possibility we are not even burdened by this question anymore. This reeks of pride. This form of arrogance is why there are so often whole ranges of "mountains" separating those sitting just one pew apart! Sometimes I wonder if we even want the mountains moved. It is, of course, easier to just do nothing. We could just sit there (cue sermon on apathy). But when we do, we miss everything!

These thoughts are not so much a call to The Great Commission,[5] but are more of an identification of a potential impediment to what should be our unquestionable, undebatable priority and standard (which would be The Great Commission). The impediment is our lack of brokenness before God. While the symptoms may take on various forms of sinful attitudes and behavior, the root of the problem can be found simply in that we have forgotten our need for Him.

It is my heartfelt prayer that, together with me, you would seek the desperation and brokenness of that day when there was no other hope but Jesus. Whether our lives or attitudes indicate it or not, He is still and always will be the only hope we have! So, stay broken.

CHAPTER 1

Broken

An examination of aspects of personal testimony. Acknowledging the idolatry of self-worship, the destructiveness of self-will and the desperation which leads the unregenerate to cry out the Lord.

"For we ourselves also were sometimes foolish, disobedient, deceived, serving diverse lusts and pleasures, living in malice and envy, hateful and hating one another. But after that the kindness and love of God our Savior toward man appeared."- Titus 3:3, 4

On Sunday mornings when I stand in the pulpit, all it takes is about one yawn or one glance at a watch to break my heart. I mean, it *really rattles* me. This is not because we can't deal with a little distraction. (A couple years teaching and preaching in the nursing home is great training for that.) It is also not because of some demand for respect or personal attention.

The burden of my heart in these moments is simply because the truth of the Word changed my life. Period. I wasn't a kind of decent guy who had a few questions about God, found his way to the Church and got saved. I am the biggest schmuck you'll ever meet. I was so far gone, so completely hopeless, such a hard headed and hearted case that there was no way in the world some "God" could do anything with me. I couldn't live successfully and I couldn't die and I didn't care much about either. I hated the words "Church," "God," "Jesus," "Spirit" and most of all "Bible." And then one day, broken and desperate (more desperate at the time not over death but over just the prospect of five more minutes of life in that condition), I encountered Jesus. I encountered the Living Word. That day—my life and my eternity were transformed.

The verses mentioned in the heading of this chapter are a snapshot testimony of every true believer. While the details of our testimonies may vary, the general characteristics of "lost-ness" are universal. I have recently taken to using the list of characteristics of who we once were from Titus 3:3 for a type of "historical examination exercise." I begin by meditating upon the characteristic of "lostness" as listed in Scripture (foolishness, for example). I then reflect upon what specific behaviors of my past resemble that characteristic according to how Scripture defines it (foolishness as described in Psalm 14:1). Here's why.

I have found a profound usefulness in regularly (some might even suggest daily) reaching back to that time before Christ and to touch intimately the pain of that lost condition. This is not to wallow in the past or to beat myself up with remorse and guilt over the sin for which I have been forgiven. (We all know self-pity and self-deprecation are just forms of self-centeredness right?) It is to remember how desperate I was that day. How I'd have done anything to be delivered from that broken state and how I joyfully found I didn't have to do anything at all. I simply had to accept what had already been done for me. At that moment, desperation and brokenness became no longer a weakness, but a conduit to the awesome power of God at work in my life.

-Creating God-

"For we ourselves also were sometimes foolish."

I think "sometimes" is generous. I know the NIV translates this as "were once," and it is a reflection upon who we were before Christ, but I still get a chuckle out of it every time I read it in the King James. That certainly is how I would have described myself. "Brilliant with occasional lapses into foolish behavior." Truth is, according to Scripture, I was an idiot.

Since I already mentioned Psalm 14:1, let's start there. *"The fool hath said in his heart that there is no God."* This doesn't necessarily mean that I didn't think God existed at all, it was just that I wanted to be the one to define Him. This is at the core of the nature of idolatry.[1] I spent years gathering the proverbial wood, clay, silver and gold, and fashioned God into who I wanted Him to be. God made in my image. Like I said—idiot.

The problem I found with this "god" that I had created was that, much like myself, he failed quite often. He was undependable, dishonest and generally a pretty big disappointment. Since he seemed so indifferent to my causes, conditions and requests, I began to disregard continually the notion of God altogether. I mean, what difference did it make how I lived if God didn't care one way or the other? Since he (this god of my own making) was neither a help nor a hindrance, why regard him at all? So, in my heart I said, "there is no God."

It's not that I had never been introduced to the God of the Bible. When I was a kid, we went to Church. We were "decent" people. But whether the point of it all was clearly stated or not, I definitely missed it. As soon as I was old enough to get away with not going (for me that was about 14), I didn't.

-Rebellion-

"Disobedient."

When I glance over my shoulder from today and I recall eventually giving up on the idea of God, I remember vividly the underlying hopelessness which accompanied that heart. You see, what preceded this giving up on God was giving up on myself. As I spiraled through a life of dissatisfaction and unrealized potential, I saw my efforts were failing to change both myself and my circumstances. "God" was the straw that I began to grasp at, but as was already stated, I was definitely going to tell Him what He needed to do and how He needed to do it. (I cringe today when our petitions and requests before the throne resemble more dictations and demands.)

The reason why is because I never saw much use in taking direction from anyone. Don't get me wrong, I'd follow the rules to stay under the radar. I'd "behave" to access positions of privilege and self-serving notoriety.

But when I did what was right, I almost always did it for the wrong reasons. I was a five-year-old kid (and really never grew up much from there) walking around with a God complex. I didn't think I knew everything, but I definitely knew more than everyone else. So why, other than to get people off my back and make my life a little easier, should I take direction or orders from anyone? I was rebellious to my core.

As time progressed in my life, the failure of this disobedient nature became increasingly apparent. It's not that I didn't have moments of "success" and "achievement," but the self-destructiveness of arrogance and pride kept me from lasting progress and realized potential. Naturally (and unfortunately quite slowly), I began to suspect that I might possibly not be all that I imagined myself to be. As the failures of life began to pile up, it cast a gloomy shadow over the brilliance I had once so strongly believed was emanating from my life. For me, these failures revealed themselves and accelerated through various addictions, but the root of the issue was always founded in the disobedience of pride and self-service. Ah, yes, it certainly *does "goeth before destruction."*[2]

I finally came to the place where I consigned myself to the hopelessness and misery of an existence of half-hearted efforts (because I knew things would eventually fall apart) and half-realized goals. It was completely unsatisfying, yet for a long time I sought satisfaction down this hopeless road.

-The Deceiver-

"Deceived, serving diverse lusts and pleasures."

I was never really a "The Devil made me do it" kind of guy. I had way too much pride to acknowledge anyone's control in or over my life. But, man, oh man, did he have me hooked and swindled. The *"god* [lower case g, Satan] *of this world"*[3] had me so blind that for the longest time I believed with the deepest of conviction that I could find some way out of my misery. Somehow, some way, I thought, the road of the search for self-satisfaction would lead me to peace.

Since I fancied myself at one time the wisest person in the world (a legend in my own mind), I have always been able to relate pretty well to Solomon. The early verses of Ecclesiastes identify all the different ways that Solomon sought meaning and satisfaction from life. The various pursuits of laughter, lust, liquor, learning and labor turned out to be useless in the endeavor to find meaning in life for him.[4] (I don't know who came up with the five L's, but I'm giving them credit here.)

I too sought to shrug everything away as no big deal as I recall my grunge phase (man, I looked great in flannel and ripped jeans). At times, I fancied myself an intellectual as I snoozed my way through P.D. Ouspensky (a philosopher) and the like. My greed promoted exertions and energies into various financial pursuits, and I certainly sought fulfillment through the physical and psychological satisfaction that came from the attention of the opposite sex. As I have already mentioned, addictions of many types became a hallmark of my life and eventually consumed virtually every aspect of it.

As I look back, I see that these useless "satisfaction endeavors" were not totally useless, for through them I began to see how trapped I was by the pursuits that had come to dominate me. The financial pride that drove me to keep up with the Smiths (the Joneses moved away after I passed out in their yard too many times) kept me working long hours and exhausted. My addictions (often spurred on by my desire to endure more work), grew ever worse as my family and jobs suffered, and just made everything I tried to do more difficult. I had become a slave to my desires and came to a place that when I tried to walk away from them, I was entirely unable to do so.

Let me take a moment to say that addiction is a particularly cruel device of the Enemy. It not only causes one to destroy blindly their own life, but it destroys anyone else in the blast radius of it. The closer someone is to the addict, the deeper they are hurt, the more severe the scars and the longer the damage lasts. It is self-centered behavior in its purest form--so severe that the addicted are rarely even aware of the devastating effect their behavior and choices are having on others.

I spent years of my life chasing the elusive deliverance[5] I believed could be found in the bottle, pill, needle or pipe. This pursuit took me to the darkest corners of depravity and desperation. I arrived quickly and remained in the place, where I would do anything or be anyone as I was *"drawn away of my own lusts."*[6] The continual fog of intoxication mixed with the darkness of my hopeless condition became a cocktail which so inebriated my heart and mind that suicide was continually contemplated and occasionally (in earnest) attempted. Lock-down rehabs and mental institutions became a sad reality.

Many times I tried to run away from myself, but wherever I arrived, I always found the same person there, just in an ever-worsening condition. My exploits found me on one occasion in a sanitarium (mental-institution) in central Mexico. I spent most of my half-year there tied to a bed with rope, screaming at the ceiling.

Today I try very purposefully not to glorify in any way the situations to which my choices brought me. There are certainly some stories of my past which are slightly humorous because of the extreme stupidity involved in my actions. However, any part of my history I share with others is done so with one purpose in mind. I want people to know what the Lord has done and what He can do.

You see, I need always remember where *my* individual choices, efforts, intellect and ideas will lead me. It must be understood that the very best we can do for ourselves apart from Jesus Christ is an eternity in the lake of fire. The broken condition of "lost" in whatever way we have experienced it in our lives is a glimpse (*just a glimpse*) of the eternity of suffering, sorrow and torment which awaits all who are apart from His redeeming grace. The very best I can do on my own is tied down to bed in a Mexican mental-institution screaming at the ceiling. Kind of makes me want to depend on Him.

-Misery-

"Living in malice and envy, hateful and hating one another."

It almost goes without saying that because of the aspects of pride which were such a part of my life, for a long time I viewed my difficulties and struggles as not my fault but someone else's. The above Scripture illustrates two dynamics that go along with this false idea I had as to my unsatisfactory condition. First, because my dissatisfaction was the product (I thought) of external circumstances, over time I began to develop an extreme dislike for people in general. After all, it was *their fault* things were working out for me the way they were so why should I like them? Unaddressed dislike and anger will eventually develop into all-out resentment as it did for me, and the resting place of that resentment was hatred. I hated everyone and, finally, I hated myself.

To make matters worse (yes, it gets worse) my eye, which was rarely on myself and almost always turned toward others, would jealously look toward all the "green grass" on the other side of the fence. Everyone, it seemed, had it better than I did. I was perpetually plagued with deep self-pity. In my anger over my failing condition and my hatred toward other people and circumstances for "causing" it, I began to seek to maliciously destroy others. I was mean, vengeful, hurtful, arrogant, slanderous and petty. The only momentary happiness I could find toward the end was when someone else failed and I had something to do with it.

Directly in the cross hairs of all of these blasphemous, rebellious, bewildered, hateful attitudes was the Body of Jesus Christ. I really couldn't stand Christians. With their joy and their peace. Please. Their purpose and selflessness. That Bible that they trusted in so much. Come on.

I realize not all professing believers carry these qualities. There are, after all, many make- believers out there. But the true believers do. I encountered so many true believers who tried to love me when I insulted them, who tried to welcome me when I mocked them, who tried to witness to me when I belittled them[7]—and then they *still* kept coming back for more! You know, Jesus loves the hard case.[8] I get a little misty-eyed when I think of the kind of things people around me needed to endure because the Lord was longsuffering with me. I'm sure they would say it was worth it, but still it amazes me to this day.

When I encounter the man who was instrumental in leading me to Christ (one of the ones who endured a whole lot from me), I always try to take a little encouraging poke at him:

If anyone else is standing around, I'll say "That's the man who told me about Jesus!"

"So it's *your* fault," I've heard some people say to him.

Brother Darold will almost always reply in my direction, "I couldn't *not* tell you about Jesus…"

What a response.

-The Moment-

"But after that the kindness and love of God our Savior toward man appeared."

So there I was. All the foolishness, disobedience, blindness and hatred leading to that one day that finally gave way to total and complete hopelessness. Emptiness. Barrenness. To the terrible realization that my way of doing things and looking at things would never, ever work. Finally, I had no fight left in me. No excuses or blames left. No more brilliant schemes and no way out. *I was broken.*

I remember dragging myself through that day. I was residing in the 16th institution into which I had checked myself, a small half-way house out in the country. I didn't want to go because "they made you sit in those stupid Bible studies," but I didn't have anywhere else to go so I went. It was a Friday. I had worked up a plan to score some dope just to make the pain a little less for a little while. As I was preparing to throw away yet another chance at getting some help, a miracle occurred. God intervened, *and I saw it.*

The plan I had concocted fell apart and I saw for the first time that it wasn't circumstance or happenstance that caused the failed plan, but I *knew* that it was an intervention of the Almighty God—that my plan had gotten in the way of His plan and His was bigger than mine. In that instant, I saw as I looked back over the course of my miserable life, that time and time again God had pushed me, pulled me, nudged me, shoved me and carried me to bring me to that day and that moment. My heart saw the tears in His eyes as he watched me destroy myself and my heart heard the words of my Savior say, "Son, if you only knew!"[9] Realizing in that moment that His kindness had moved me from no hope to one, in desperation and broken, I fell to my knees and cried out to the only Hope there was:

"Lord, I can't do anything right. I can't do anything on my own. I am totally hopeless. You are my only Hope. Please rescue me from my hopelessness. Please help me. Please forgive me. Please save me. In Jesus name."

No preacher saying, "repeat after me." No Roman Road. (I was familiar with the Gospel because of all those persistent seed-planters.) No ABC's. Just a hopeless idiot throwing himself in desperation before the Lord.

CHAPTER 2

The Power of Brokenness

**Acknowledging the liberating and powerful
value of the desperate moment when the
unregenerate cry out to the Lord. The
immediate operation of the power of the
Holy Spirit in the life of the reborn.**

*"Not by works of righteousness which we have
done, but according to his mercy he saved us,
by the washing of regeneration, and renewing of
the Holy Ghost; which he shed on us abundantly
through Jesus Christ our Savior." - Titus 3:5,6*

I have been tempted to wonder through the course
of this project, "Do I have the kind of credibility and
credentials necessary to share these burdens and be

heard?" I'm a relatively young man. I haven't been in the ministry very long. I don't pastor a mega church.

The Enemy would have me say, "No," but here's what I know (Get behind me Satan). Any credibility I have, and ever will, lies in Christ. My credentials are written in the power of His shed blood and the power of His Word applied to my pathetic life. Many preachers (myself included) love to reflect upon the boldness of the Apostles as they stood before the Sanhedrin in Acts 4:13. Peter and John spoke so confidently from the Old Testament text, and through it, revealed Christ. Their statements were qualified not by their training, eloquence or social standing. They were qualified by the fact that "*they had been with Jesus.*"

Please understand: I love to study. My library grows nearly daily. I am surrounded by incredible formal educators and gifted, experienced pastors who've taken pity on me and have blessed me with their time. Yet, may it never be said of any of us that we are who we are because of our efforts or aptitudes. May the most noticeable characteristic of what has been produced from our lives always be that it came because we have "*been with Jesus.*" That is my prayer.

-All His Doing-

"Not by works of righteousness which we have done, but according to His mercy he saved us."

As I think back to that broken day when everything changed, I am amazed still at how absolutely nothing I had to do with it. I am fond of calling it "the sovereign symphony of God." How beautifully He orchestrated the exact set of circumstances that brought me to the moment in which I called upon Him.[1] Think about it with me for a minute.

Every person we meet, every situation we encounter, every circumstance we create affects us in either a positive or negative way. The Lord both wrote and calculated the perfect equation to where all the pluses and minuses of my life added up to both the broken state I was in and the glimmer of hope that followed. In His preemptive and omniscient mercy, He had already gone to the cross, died in payment for my sin, and rose so it would be possible to apply the work of the cross to my life. He then ascended into heaven and, on that broken day, the Father sent the Spirit through the Son to reprove the hopelessness in me and its cause (sin). Finally, the same Spirit led me to repentance[2] in turning to Him as

17

my only hope. Wow. And that's just the tiny little part of all of it He's allowed me to see!

It was all His righteous work and none of mine. This divine work was and is so far out of my league, so far out of my jurisdiction.

Whenever I teach the parable of the fig tree in Luke 13:6-9, there is a particular point I always try to make. You remember the story Christ told: He had been teaching about the need for repentance in light of the "perishing" that awaits all who don't. He then followed these warnings with the story of a man who had a fig tree in a garden. The man had been waiting for the fig tree to produce fruit, and it had not, so he encourages the gardener to cut it down. The gardener desires to fertilize the tree to give it another opportunity to bear fruit before it is cut down. (Is this the part of the story I'm supposed to relate to? I'm the fertilizer right? Maybe not.) End of story.

Since the parable is preceded by a call to repentance, it is understood by many that repentance is the sought after "fruit" by the "owner of the garden" and the "gardener." The point I mentioned earlier (the one I always try to emphasize) is that the fig tree has only one thing to do. The tree is not asked to weigh in on the state of affairs of the garden. He's not asked for his opinion or to make any decisions regarding itself. The fig tree has exactly one job: Make a fig. Message: In light of the imminent chopping down there's one thing to do—repent!

This is some of that "Jesus rocket science" I love so much. He breaks it down to where even I can understand it: Good tree. Good fruit. Bad tree. Bad fruit. Good tree—no bad fruit. Bad tree—no good fruit.[3] I love it.

When my eyes were opened to the previously mentioned sovereign symphony of circumstance, and I saw there was only one alternative to misery and perishing, I took it. I recall that broken day as I look to this parable and rejoice in the understanding that was revealed: Respond to all the effort and patience of the "owner" and "the gardener." Recognize there was one alternative to the demise that loomed before me and repent. But can the fig tree really take credit for the production of the fruit? Could I act like or consider that *I'd* accomplished something when I turned to Him in desperation and He saved me? I think not. His work, His effort, and His patience delivered me. Nothing more.

-Holy Spirit!-

"By the washing of regeneration and renewing of the Holy Ghost."

When I arose (I've got to use the word "arose" at least one time) from my knees the day I cried out to Him, I really didn't "feel" very different. I was, after all, in the same body. It was a body that had been wracked with pain, guilt, remorse, sorrow, addiction and futility for years. I was still dope sick. I was still broke financially. (Actually, I'd managed to work myself a good distance into the red.) You know, I'd spent a great deal of my life trying to change my circumstances and surroundings and after throwing myself down before the Lord, my circumstances and surroundings hadn't changed a bit. I can't testify as to the weight of the world being lifted off my shoulders or a tremendous release of some kind having taken place. (I'm still searching the pages of Scripture today to find where the "life-is-a-rose-garden-and-Jesus-will-make-all-your-problems-go-away" doctrine came from.) But I *can* testify.

It was an interesting "coincidence" that at the moment I got up from my knees (I mean arose) and walked from the room I had been crying, snotting, and praying in, it happened to be time for a Bible study. You know, those Bible studies that I called "stupid" which were the main reason I didn't want to come to that particular half-way house. I walked into the room, sat down, opened the book and began to listen to the man as he taught.

Let me take just a moment in case I haven't emphasized the point enough, to say that for most of my adult life I really, really, really, didn't like the Bible. I didn't own one, didn't want one, and sure didn't want to hear you quoting one. I fumed when I heard those words "the Bible says…" Ugh.

So, I sat in that room and heard the Word. But now, something was different. Up to that moment, the Word of God sounded to me like fingernails on a chalkboard. But now, in a great miracle of His grace, it became the Word of God *to me*. I heard it not only as His message but His personal message to me. Just a few moments before, God had allowed me a glimpse of the sovereign symphony He had orchestrated which brought me to my knees. Now I had a chance to hear the beautiful sound of His "music." I was like a deaf man hearing for the first time. My heart burned. My eyes watered. The truth began to wash over me like a cool shower as the "living water" welled up within—springing up in confirmation of the relationship that had been established with Him.

I can't remember the text that the leader taught from that night, but I remember the subject. The subject was what it should always be: Jesus. And as that man taught me about Jesus that night, he made a statement that has rung in my ears ever since. He said, "I wake up every morning in desperate need of help." This was coming from a man who had walked with the Lord for decades—someone I had always identified as a strong person. But he understood where every ounce of his strength came from—he understood that he would *always* be desperate for Jesus.

At times today, we are given the reminiscent grace to recall just how much of nothing we are apart from Him. It is then when we become open vessels into which His amazing power can be poured once again. That was, after all, the beginning point of His power working in our lives, wasn't it? It was only when we saw that we were hopeless, that we were then able to see that there was hope in Him and were prepared to receive the power of that hope as well.

It was upon the reception of the power of hope in Christ that my circumstances and surroundings began to change. Now, they didn't change because the Lord zapped them different or away. Things began to change because in brokenness and abandon before Him He enabled me to begin to live differently (which will consequentially begin to change many of our circumstances and surroundings.) Simultaneously (what a conductor He is!), as I began to see the power of God transforming my life, my *perspective* began to change as well. Instead of seeing the hopelessness and overwhelming aspects of the various places and predicaments I was in, I began to see the potential and the possibilities. I began to truly believe that it was possible through this amazing God that I might not have to keep struggling with the same burdens and mistakes over and over again.

This possibility caused a tremendous stirring within me to seek a fervent dependence upon God (always with the shadow of my track record of self-dependence looming in the background). And, because I had experienced this conviction through an encounter with His Word, it was consequential that I would exercise my dependence upon Him through reliance upon His Word. Again, it was not a matter of an effort of altering my perspectives and revealing new ones, but the grace of the Lord sharing His perspectives with me.

One aspect of the early days that followed that blessed, broken, day of redemption often comes to mind. I had been attending Bible study and church and was thrilled with the fulfillment I was finding in what I had before found neither interesting nor useful. Along the way, however, there were days of discouragements, setbacks and anxieties which I would frequently encounter. Remember, there is a very real adversary who wants us to fail as believers so the Lord won't be glorified.[4] The hail of fiery[5] darts was overwhelming to me as the Enemy sought to tempt me away from the dependence I had found to be so powerful. To tempt me to re-purchase the lie which had been discarded and defeated—that I, through my *own efforts,* could work my way out of these situations.[6] As that strong recollection as to what I had previously achieved through personal effort (not a whole lot) began to well up from within, desperation began to set in.

On one of these such days, in a glorious moment of conviction, I reached into my pocket and pulled out the little Bible I had been putting there every day since I had received it. (Go Gideons! Go Gideons!) I was faltering. I was desperate. I needed God's help. I prayed, "Help me. Please." And I *opened His Word.*

Today, I try to encourage people to include some aspects of structure in their personal Bible study—to use all the resources, helps and counsel available. To not always use the "My-Bible-fell-open-to-this-page-so-this-is-the-one-I'm-supposed-to-read" approach. To be the best student of the Word we can be and to seek to grow in knowledge and application of the whole counsel of God's Word.

Having said that, on *that* day I just straight up stuck my thumb on a page, opened it and read what it said. Here I was about to fly apart, feeling especially weak in the moment and I had miraculously turned to 2 Timothy, Chapter 2. Check this out. *"Thou therefore*

*my son be strong in the grace that is in Christ Jesus...
Thou therefore endure hardness as a good soldier of
Jesus Christ."*

On that day, the Lord reminded me through His
Word that my strength would come not through my
effort, but by His grace. I was totally dependent upon
Him for it. I was further reminded that as a soldier
who belonged to Him, I was capable of enduring
hardness victoriously. I wasn't just reading inspirational
words. I was reading Words that were *inspired*! The
breath of God resuscitated my failing heart. Matter of
fact, the Word of God was laid upon my heart like a
defibrillator, and I think I might have even heard Him
say "Clear." Zap!

-This Stuff Works-

*"Which he shed on us abundantly through Jesus
Christ our Savior."*

I began to wonder if it could always be like this
with His Word. With each new challenge I encountered,
every decision and question I faced, I sought more and
more to find the answers and direction in Scripture. In
His sovereign grace, when I decided not to consult His
Word, I would experience the familiar bewilderment

of the self-propelled life once again. There have been those times when Scripture was naïvely misapplied. The products of these forays (thankfully) are never what a true representation of Scripture should be and are readily identifiable when we are simply willing to consider we may not always be right. (More on the humility aspect of brokenness later.)

More and more as I stumbled my way along with the *"lamp and light"*[7] in hand, I became convinced of the one simple fact which has come to define the action of my walk with Christ—*This stuff really works!*[8] The simple, systematic and earnest application of His Truth would change my life so that I might walk in the power I had encountered on that day when I had nowhere to turn but to Jesus.

So, here I am today, nearly a decade later, still convinced about the transforming power of the Truth— still convinced that as we yield ourselves to that Truth in broken, desperate abandon, the power of the Holy Spirit of God will illuminate that Truth that we might utilize it for His glory. It is the great weapon in our lives with which to battle the works of Satan. Indeed, the Word was made manifest[9] that Satan's works might be destroyed![10]

It is one of the clearest expressions of brokenness that can come forth from the life of the believer—to be sold-out, dependent and desperate for His Word. Time and time again, the testimony of the Word and the testimony of His Saints reveal that when people are broken before Him and turn to the Word, miraculous things occur.

"For the preaching of the cross is to them that perish foolishness; but unto us which are saved it is the power of God." - 1 Corinthians 1:18

CHAPTER 3

Returning to Brokenness

**Acknowledging the susceptibility believers have
to wander away from the powerful brokenness
of the day of justification. Accepting the fact
that in some way, we already *have* wandered.
Repenting and the joyful guarantee of
acceptance when we turn back to the Lord.**

*"The sacrifices of God are a broken spirit:
a broken and contrite heart, O God, thou
wilt not despise." - Psalm 51:17*

Press on. Remember. Be diligent. Beware. Scripture
is full of warnings, exhortations and reminders to
remember who we are (nothing apart from Him[1]) and
all that God has done for us. In the wake of this potential

"forgetfulness" are a multitude of the sinful behaviors common to man. It seems the more forgetful we are of God's grace and provision, the more frequent and grievous the sin. One of the things which believers (myself included) have a very hard time admitting and coming to regular terms with, is that we all are absolutely susceptible to this type of forgetful behavior and the subsequent sin. (Who me? Surely not!—I love how often people walk out of the church and say "Pastor, I know someone who really needed to hear that message!" Yeah, so do I.)

Scripture repeatedly acknowledges this challenge of admission. While I never present this as some kind of universal principle, it can be generally understood that there is a direct correlation between the frequency of scriptural admonitions on a subject and the severity of man's struggle to come to terms with it.[2] In the light of this understanding—*we stink at remembering what God has done for us and how much we need Him.*

The Lord (thankfully) is fully aware of the "quick forgetters" we carry around on our shoulders. He knows we need to be reminded. This is why we have so many records in Scripture of people forgetting the works of the Lord, the subsequent consequences, and the progress of the Lord wrought when His people acknowledge Him. In regard to the specific struggles of Israel in the wilderness mentioned in 1 Corinthians 10, the Lord's intention for this record of Scripture is for us to learn from the record that we (the Church) might not *"lust after"*[3] the same evil things. Jeremiah delivered the same type of reminder to Judah using the defeat of Israel as his example in Jeremiah 3:6, 7.

Isn't it funny how we sit in Sunday School (or small group on Tuesday) and are so amazed at the short-sightedness and lack of fortitude we find among God's people in the pages of the Old Testament?

"Those people hadn't been delivered from Pharaoh's army for barely three days, and they started complaining!"[4]

"How could David have done such a thing after all God had done for him?!"[5]

"Why in the world would those people come back to Jerusalem and beautify their houses instead of rebuilding the Temple?"[6]

We sit there with all the appropriate amazement at the nature of sinful man. We'll even give the appropriate lip-service as to how quickly *we* complain and lose gratitude (yes, I'll call it lip-service because *"Godly sorrow sorrows to repentance"*).[7] We may even acknowledge a transgression ("I've got some work to do in that area, but I'm only human."…more on that later). But the lack of brokenness and desperation we

31

have over even *the potential* that we are engaged in the same neglectfulness as Scriptures' examples leaves us sitting there looking like we believe that half of us are named Caleb and the other half Joshua![8]

Perhaps an example from the Epistles will help illustrate this point further. In Galatians Chapter 2 is the record of an altercation between Paul and Peter. Years before, Peter had been used of God to carry the Gospel to the Roman Cornelius. The grand principle taught to Peter through the process of his interaction with Cornelius came directly from the Lord Himself: *"What God hath cleansed, that call not thou uncommon."*[9] Ephesians confirms for us that it is the Gospel which has *"broken down the middle wall of partition"*[10] between Jew and Gentile.

Yet, in a later time when Peter was in Antioch of Syria, he was reluctant to interact with the Gentile converts of the Church in the presence of Jewish converts who were holding to a false, works-based gospel. His actions said he'd forgotten what the Lord had shown him! To make matters worse, this forgetfulness was influencing other members of the body. Barnabas is even mentioned among those who were engaged in this hypocrisy. Now, Barnabas wasn't some shmo who just didn't know nothing. He was a front-line warrior of the Gospel. Yet they forgot, in essence, the truth of the gospel itself! Well, here then comes Paul, all up in Peter's face and calling him out for his hypocrisy. Now that's inspirational stuff: Taking a stand for the Gospel of Jesus Christ! Taking a stand even when it's unpopular or puts us in the minority among other believers.

I get some pretty high raises of eyebrows when I am among believers and I make mention of the fact that we're *all* a bit deluded about the quality of our Christian walk in some way. We want so desperately to identify with Paul in this encounter don't we? But let's get real. How many times have we acted more like Peter and less like Paul in similar situations? Our youth groups aren't the only ones who need to hear messages about peer pressure and going along with the crowd. How often do our actions betray the truth of the Gospel we claim (and yes, seek) to uphold?

The degree of cultivation in our character will always be revealed when we examine the evidence of the times we've been "squeezed" in our walk with the Lord. Those times when to do what's right is to do what is uncomfortable, painful or costly. Sometimes we do great (Glory to God). Sometimes we do not. The question is should "sometimes" ever be good enough? Will the life of the believer who settles for "good enough" produce an extraordinary witness for Him? *Does it honestly matter to me if my life does?*

These kinds of tough questions are never for the purpose of beating ourselves up. Please don't do that— it's one of the ways Satan tempts the believer into inactivity. Tough questions like these are always for the purpose of exposing how quickly and easily we can get away from what we truly believe *that we might return desperately to what we believe once again!*

-Admission-

"The sacrifices of God are a broken Spirit."

Admission, (as always) is the first step in the process. Daily, constantly, I have to admit I am susceptible to taking steps away from the Lord. Any honest assessment of our deportment will reveal that we are not only capable of these wayward steps, but we have taken several too.[11] Until we acknowledge this constant peril, our walk will not be circumspect. If we think a car will never come down the road, why would we look both ways before crossing the street? The reality is we are standing on the side of the proverbial interstate and the only hope to get across is holding His hand.

Sometimes the Lord allows wonderful little experiences into our lives to teach us those lessons we so need to learn. One day a few years ago when my youngest son was quite little, we were arriving at the grocery store for a shopping trip. It was just around the time when my son wasn't holding our hands in all situations and times anymore. Even though we weren't holding hands at that moment, he was hanging pretty close by my side as we left the parked car and headed to the entrance. As we approached the high traffic driveway between the parking lot and the building, the little guy made a little motion that spoke volumes to me.

Without looking both ways and without looking up at me, without any prompting, direction or warning at all, he simply reached up for my hand. He was nearing a place where his experience had told him (this was not his first trip to the grocery store) he was potentially in peril. He had come to accept he needed help and trusted that the help would not only be there, but that it would bring him safely to the other side of the driveway. He also had probably watched enough Wile E. Coyote cartoons to envision a little boy-shaped pancake on the asphalt too.

I'm sure further interpretation is unnecessary. Wouldn't it be so appropriate for us to venture forward as believers with this kind of needy perspective and trust as well? Are we willing to ask ourselves if our lives truly reflect this kind of dependence and faith? Sometimes it just doesn't.

We develop this form of spiritual jay-walking when *we* increase and God decreases.[12] It develops when the achievements and victories won in the life of the believer by the Lord and His power subtly parlay into faith in oneself: we think, "I've got this Jesus thing now." (Yikes!) If we were to say it out loud, we would immediately hear the ridiculousness of it all. Once again however, our actions betray the faith we proclaim. Our actions often say the object of our faith is our own selves! Accepting the fact that we exercise this form of hypocrisy *regularly* is one of the toughest Christian pills to swallow. None of us likes to think of our faith as small. None of us likes to consider aspects of hypocrisy in our walk with the Lord. But we must come clean before Him if we are to be cleansed! *"And everyman that hath this hope in him purifieth himself even as he is pure."*[13]

How often have we heard (and said), "Jesus said all it takes is faith the size of a mustard seed."[14] Well, thus saith the Lord and no question about it. There is amazing power in faith. This is encouraging news about this mustard seed indeed. But, shouldn't it also be considered that this truth is set before us not only to show us how great the power is in a small amount of faith but also to show us *how small amount of faith we have*? How often do we *not* see mountains moving around us?

Our lack of desperate, continual brokenness is the cause of this hypocrisy. *And it is not a simple fix.* In fact, if we're being honest, the best we can do is to make progress. But the progress is so worth it because with this kind of progress comes a return to the power which miraculously alters everything—which moves mountains! Losing faith in one's self is not an event. It must be viewed as a constant process in the life of the believer.

-Repentance-

"A broken and contrite heart."

Most of the time, when we look to Christ's Parable of the Wayward Son[15] (of course, a favorite of mine) we think about a troubled friend or family member. Perhaps a member of our church who had made poor choices and is no longer around. (Pastor, I know someone who really needed to hear that message…) We might recall a time in our past when our lives were shattered, and we turned or returned to Him. It is actually in this way that I have always looked at this parable: a fond recollection of a past victory of God. Might I submit for our consideration that this parable is a parable for *every believer every day*?

Recall the parable together with me. The younger of two sons prematurely asks for his inheritance from his father. The father grants the request, and the son takes his inheritance and squanders it. Through the process of experiencing the consequences of his squandering, the younger son realizes both his undesirable condition and recalls the kind of security and provision that all enjoyed back at his father's house. With an attitude that is notably different from the one he had when he left (broken, desperate and repentant), he decides to return to the father. His hope is simply some measure of acceptance, but as we recall the father welcomes him back fully as his son. They throw a party. Awesome stuff.

Again, our constant application of this text seems to be for the young adult in their late twenties who left the church after they were "enlightened" at college and had now returned. For the guy or gal who started drinking and had come back to the church in the hope of straightening up. In no way do I refute these applications. But what about our times of wavering faithfulness, disgruntled service, words which don't edify and selfish actions we perform when no one's looking? Don't we "walk off the farm" when we are engaged in these behaviors as well? Frankly, how low do we really want to set the bar when it comes to acceptable levels of sin? Is there such a thing?

Every day in some way we squander our relationship with the Lord. We squander our inheritance. Every day there is some opportunity that stands *"unredeemed."*[16] Why, oh why, is it so hard for us to smell the stench of the hog pen in our nostrils? Have we been so influenced by the "Febreze" of religious motion and attendance that we really, truly believe we're pretty much on track and doing okay most of the time? Do we feel as if we remain in the perpetual state of attending the return party? ("Oh, look, they're throwing a party for me again today!")

I've said it so many times and have heard it as well. "Jesus is my everything. I owe it all to Him!" How often do our schedules, bank accounts and hearts betray these statements? Once again, this is not a self-bashing session. But we have got to get real and keep it real if we're going to walk in the revolutionary and transforming power we encountered the day we were apprehended by Christ. Every day, constantly, we need to *"arise and go to the father."*

-Acceptance-

"Oh God, thou wilt not despise."

So, if we're willing to accept the possibility that we are not as nigh unto the Lord[17] as we previously believed we were, what is God looking for from us when we return to Him? We know He's looking. We know He's expecting. We know He's waiting. We love the idea—the truth—of this Father of the wayward son awaiting the arrival of the son back to his home.

"Okay," we tell ourselves, "so I'm coming back to God. I'm going to start studying more, start serving more, start praying more, start giving more, start showing up for more. I'm going to 'do' for God!"

This is the first mistake we so often make in the midst of a willingness to take a good hard look at ourselves. You see, as believers, we are frequently so focused with "doing" that which is pleasing to God. "Lord, help us to *do* that which is pleasing in your sight." And then we start *doing*. Stuff. Things. Yes many good things, but still—things. Isn't that where the whole problem started? Didn't we learn sometime in the unfortunately musty past that there is nothing we can do to earn our way to God? Our mistake is that we try to correct our course with action. Don't get me wrong, we have certainly got to be a "doing" people. But while we "do" *for* Him as a response to His grace, we can never "do" *to* Him to earn that grace.

The wayward son couldn't go make things right with his father. He couldn't restore the inheritance he'd squandered. He was slap broke, remember? All he had to carry up the road was his broken, desperate, pitiful self. He had some hope too. He never would have gotten up and returned to the father if there wasn't a chance he'd allow him to return. Notice that this was all the father required! Imagine if he came bearing gifts: "Here dad, I'm sorry for wasting all your money, but I brought you a nice pile of steaming pig poop to make up for it." Get the picture?

All he wants is you. This is awesome news! At the risk of taking too much exegetical liberty with this parable, I really like to think that this kid was barely a half a foot away from the hog pen when the expectant father began to run to him.

The Lord will not regard it lightly when we acknowledge our helplessness is earning a return trip to Him—when we acknowledge our complete dependence upon Him for restoration, progress and the power to accomplish either. Joyfully, as believers, there will be plenty of time and opportunity for works based upon our faith where we can show what we believe and who we trust with what we do.[18] But every action and breath must be so firmly rooted in the fact that none can be expended without the power and Spirit of God. This broken, total dependence is a sweet savor before the Lord. It is that which is pleasing in His sight.

"And he shall sit as a refiner and purifier of silver: and he shall purify the sons of Levi, and purge them as gold and silver, that they may offer unto the LORD an offering in righteousness. Then shall the offering of Judah and Jerusalem be pleasant unto the LORD, as in the days of old, and as in the former years."- Malachi 3:3, 4

CHAPTER 4

Broken over the Word

**Recognizing the Word of God as the essential
Message from God. The action of brokenness
exercised through dependence upon the Word.**

*"And it came to pass, when the king had
heard the words of the book of the law,
that he rent his clothes."- 2 King 22:11*

So how do we exercise this continual, broken, desperate,
dependence? While we understand that a starting
point is a form of constant acceptance of our own
inadequacies, eventually we will need to begin to do
something. Where do we go next?

We could certainly begin with prayer. Rekindling,
restoring and developing our relationship with the Lord

definitely involves communication with Him. I would never discourage someone from praying and will give due diligence to the examination of the institution of prayer in the next chapter. It is imperative that we express our desperation and dependence directly to Him who fulfills and sustains. However, I have for us what amounts to nothing more than a reflective suggestion. In light of our human propensity toward self-absorption, in light of our constant susceptibility to wander away from Him and take credit for His work, how about listening to God first and then speak? After all, whose end of the conversation do we think is most important: What we have to say or what God has to say?

-Where do we go from here?-

"And it came to pass"

So, once again, it's not so much what we *do* as it is what we *surrender to* in this walk of the broken believer. In this case, the idea is that we surrender (as a priority) to His direction, that we surrender to His Word. Scripture is the primary and most direct means of God's communication with us. We exercise our dependence upon Him through dependence upon the truth of His Word. If we have acknowledged this continual, desperate need for Him, it will stand to reason that we will not know on our own how to live out that need toward its desired consummation.

This is why the Word of God is so important. We are lost without it! Literally—it is the scripture that makes us *"wise unto salvation through faith which is in Christ Jesus."*[1] Any deliverance information of any type concerning the Lord will not be identified apart from His Word. Any deviation, distortion or omission of His truth will impede or prevent the deliverance intended through it.

It is worth noting here an event that took place in my walk with Him which was foundationally influential to how I approach teaching and preaching "messages." I will never, ever forget the day when I heard a perspective on a message from God. I was privy to a meeting of a couple ministers who were chatting about upcoming services. In the midst of this conversation, I heard a statement which punched me in my young Christian gut:

"I have the message, I just need to find some Scripture to go along with it."

Now, I don't know what is holy about molies—but holy moly!

You see, God had been speaking to me through His Word. It was literally (not theoretically or figuratively) changing my life. I was not discovering God's truth in stories, experiences, object lessons or illustrations, but in the Word itself. Of a truth—today I occasionally use an experience or an illustration to help to bring understanding to a Biblical truth, but the message from God is not the story, it is not the experience, it is not the illustration—it is the Word itself. That is God's message.

So, to deliver God's message, I can't read a section of text, close my Bible, set it aside and turn to my manuscript. Boy, am I up the creek if I attempt to do this. I might bring words that are encouraging, inspirational, instructional or even challenging, but the message from God is found in the pages of His Word.

-Listening to God-

"When the king heard"

The sovereign symphony that has brought us to share these thoughts together is again, no accident. I understand that the experience, influences and studies which the Lord has allowed into my life will not impact every person I encounter. This is, incidentally, a big challenge to come to terms with for me in the ministry. But if there is one thing that the Lord has allowed into my life, which I pray I will not cease to share with others, it is about the truth and the power of the Word. As I said earlier, *this stuff works.*

Remember, at this point in our journey of brokenness we have intimately recalled the desperation of the day of our salvation. We have also accepted the continual peril we stand in to forget both our desperate condition and the deliverance that followed. We have further acknowledged that at some point or another we have succumbed to said peril and are completely unable to work our way back to God. In re-acknowledging the desperation and brokenness which we recognize needs to be perpetually a part of our walk, we have looked for a way not to *work* back to Him, but to exercise our dependence upon Him. This has brought us face to face with the Living Word.

Regarding the exercising of this dependence, I will share with you the approach that has worked for me. I am so glad I don't have a gimmick or some "absorb-the-Bible-in-three-easy-steps" answer. Actually, the answer I found isn't mine at all. Guess where I found it? (Isn't that so much of what this kind of writing boils down to? "I'm going to write a book and I want you to read it. It's about this amazing book I found. It's called the Bible. It has all the answers we will ever need in our lives. You've got to check it out!" Kind of makes me want to take a couple chapters out so you'll get back to the Word more quickly.)

As I had mentioned in a previous chapter, very early in my walk with the Lord, I had encounters with His Word which profoundly impacted me. Having gotten a taste of the "real thing" I sought to recreate those awesome experiences through an increasing amount of time spent in the Word. Now, I understand that *I* couldn't just conjure up through my efforts a re-creating of those experiences, but more and more as I read and studied— as I yielded to His Truth, the Word was supplying those things of which I was finding myself in need. Guidance, encouragement, challenges, comfort, jolts, shake-ups, practical direction and the like poured from the Word in all its profitability.

So, this answer I found, the one about how to exercise that dependence on God—well buddy, I found it one day in Joshua 1:8, *"Meditate* [on the Word of God] *day and night."*

Of course, with this challenge, a battle between the two squirrels who always seemed to be warring in my young Christian head ensued:

"Whoa, whoa, whoa, I can't do that! Can I? Everyday?"

"Well, I thought you were *desperate...are you?*"

With this little nugget in hand (meditate day and night) which had been sprinkled with the nutty-topping (too much squirrel referencing?) of desperation, I toddled over to that shiny new concordance I had—the one that man who told me about Jesus said to buy. I found that word "meditate" can mean "to ponder." (Whew. I thought cross-legged chanting with smelly incense burning.)

In thinking of the time of the Scripture noted in the heading of this chapter, one can reflect upon the great value of this meditation. After a period of Judah wandering away from the Lord under the leadership of two disobedient kings, the young King Josiah decides to get serious about God once again.[2] He begins with the intent to accomplish a physical restoration to God's house. In the process, the people happen upon the unused, forgotten book of the law. They have an encounter with the Word. That is when the real restoration begins.

The king hears the Word and begins to ponder on what the Word says and what the implications of that Word may be. As he does, he is broken (and frightened) by the neglect of God's people in heeding the Word. Once again, this broken attitude is the one the Lord is looking for from us. It's the attitude or condition that doesn't stand in the way or refuse the work of God in someone's life. It's not that we can prevent something that is God's will to accomplish, but God will also not empower rebellion! He will not empower defiance or arrogance or pride. He will empower those of His who know and acknowledge they are powerless without Him. Listen as the Word of the Lord came to Josiah as a product of this pondering brokenness*: "Because thine heart was tender, and thou hast humbled thyself before the LORD...and hast rent thy clothes, and wept before me; I also have heard thee, saith the LORD."*[3] He will never regard it lightly when we are genuinely broken before Him!

As the Lord began to reveal this truth of His Word to me, it was then that my daily reading of the Bible began to include not only the action of reading, but also the prayerful pondering over what had been said. Time in the Word is not just a time of gathering information or a series of helpful tips. It is a time of receiving God's message.

Now, we absolutely need to study, to read and grow as we mature in our discovery of the intent of the text, context, historical background and the like. We absolutely need to ask and research that question: "Lord, what are you saying here?" But it is in the pondering upon the Word where we find the answer to the most important of questions: "Lord, what are you saying to *me*?" You see, the Bible does not just contain a "message" for us once or twice a week. It is constantly, continually, the available message from God. Anytime it is neglected, anytime is it disregarded, anytime it is not the priority for the believer, *we miss the message from God.*

Are we willing to miss His message? Can we do without it? Can I miss His message on say Monday, Tuesday and Saturday? Can we enjoy prosperity and success in defining and advancing the purpose He has for us as believers apart from the Word?

I know these kind of questions are asked all the time of believers, and we always say, "No!"...And then we come back the next Sunday and ask the same questions again. And again. And again. But often *nothing changes.* Why? Because we are not broken and desperate before Him! So we go back, all the way back *again and again*, to the day we met Jesus. We return once again to the foot of the cross. We return to the heart that knows it's hopeless apart from Him. We go back to the place where we have no answers, no solutions, no brilliant ideas. Where we were so completely bankrupt and empty we have nothing to say but "Lord, help me." And then we open His Word.

None of this denies the great value in the maturing walk of the believer or the compiling of biblical truth which is an inevitability in the life of the daily Bible student. We need not forget everything we've learned or deny the honor due the Lord for the successes and victories He's won in our process of growth in Him.

Let's not belittle what the Lord has accomplished. But the moment we start thinking "we got this thing," we will be in danger of apathy and the attitude that mediocrity is good enough.

There will always be the temptation to let up—to rely on yesterday's study, yesterday's message and yesterday's progress. It is only when we use our experience from previous instruction as a foundation for today's instruction that we will fully benefit from the value of yesterday's experiences.

-Pondering on the Word-

"The words of the book of the law"

There are some meditative practices I would like to share which are absolutely not unique, but when applied by the desperate heart, I have found them to be absolutely useful. The first one is (wait for it) read your Bible. Daily set aside time just to read. No muss, no fuss. No rushing, no going too slow. Just a continual general familiarization with the Word. Rarely do I read the books in order (certainly your prerogative to do so) but always, when coming to the close of a book, I ask simply, "Where would you have me to go next?" The more familiar we become with the Scriptures, the clearer this answer becomes based upon our needs, circumstances, or the current season of Christian service in which we are engaged.

Secondly, I routinely am always *studying* through a book as well, using the old "Strong's" and "Vine's," some good commentary and a few different translations. I chew slowly upon each verse, each truth. These are usually the truths I find myself most compelled to share with others. The more intimately familiar we are with a text, the more excited over the text we will become (even hard truths) and the more confidence we will have in recounting it. Even if it is not in a formal setting, the more we are studying with the intent to share, the more intently we will study and the more intensely a text will speak to us. It is here where the most "messages" are spoken to my heart.

Finally, there is memorization and recitation. This is hiding His Word in our hearts. It is a manner of intimacy with Scripture that I have found both liberating and powerful. The repetition of a verse over and over while going through one's day—while riding to work, while waiting in a line (perhaps silent repetition here—or not), until it becomes a part of our make-up—until it is not just something we know but it has become a notable influence upon us and a part of who we are. I remember my first real encounter with this meditative practice.

I was flipping channels as a new Christian one day and was intrigued when across the screen came the name "Friar" such-and-such. "Ok," I thought, "Let's check out the bald guy in the brown robe for a minute." I remember thinking how funny it was that this "Friar" had an accent where he sounded like he was from South Jersey. He might have even said "youze guyz" once or twice.

As I recall, this Friar was teaching from the Gospel of Matthew. I opened my Bible and began to follow along as he taught the parable from the text. Along with his interesting accent and appearance, he was also an engaging teacher and as I followed along I noticed something that is still impacting me today. This man would read a little from the Scripture and then teach on it for a minute or two. He would then continue to read and then stop and teach again. Sometimes he would read a whole verse and sometimes just a word or two as he proceeded through the text. And then I saw it. He wasn't reading his Bible!

It was open in front of him, I'm sure to the right page. But as I watched for several minutes it was obvious he wasn't reading from a teleprompter or cuecards either. *This man just knew the Scripture.* It was a part of who he was. He spoke from it and described it as if he was describing a painting he was looking at directly. Like he knew the artist, the setting, the colors and brushes that were used, and like he knew what was in the heart of the artist as he painted it. "Wow," I said, "I have got to get me some of that!"

It sounds pretty good doesn't it? Well, what's stopping you? Go to a section of Scripture which has special impact for you. (I have found this to be a useful added layer in the cake of maintaining motivation.) Write one verse down on an index card. Carry it with you everywhere you go. Just one verse. Read it and say it over and over in your heart and out loud when you can. If it takes a week to learn it, that's fine. When you know it, write the next verse down. Now you are carrying two cards, and then three and then four. Titus, for example, has 46 verses in it. In less than a year, you can have the whole book memorized!

I need to tell you that I don't ponder on the Word because I am a preacher or minister or pastor. These are important but secondary reasons for my time in the Word. Even though the service I am called to is a priority for me, it is secondary in the sense that I cannot hope to encourage and help others to apply the Scripture to their lives unless it is continually applied to my own. Before any of us can hope to sit or stand before others and influence them with Truth (every believer is a minister of reconciliation[4]), we have to be personally sold out to it.

Perhaps you are wondering if all this desperate, broken, pondering is worth it? Sometimes people still look at me like I'm crazy. Why do I so strongly believe that a continual brokenness before God and desperation for the truth of the Word is integral in the powerful and purposeful life of the believer? Well, I didn't have to smoke crack today. I didn't have to shoot heroin today. I didn't try to kill myself today, nor did I have to be committed to a mental institution today to prevent an attempt at suicide. I didn't have to steal today. I got up today from my own bed—not someone's couch, not someone's lawn furniture, not from the metal slab hanging from a wall in lock-up. I'm pretty sure I didn't run my wife off today (she's sitting on the couch reading in the living room right now), and I don't think I ran any businesses into the ground today. No one changed locks on any doors I tried to open today and at least half the people I encountered today didn't cross the street when they saw me coming (ha).

Not only did I get up from my own bed this morning, I *wanted* to get up this morning. I have people to go and see and Kingdom things to go and do. I've got Bible I want to read and people I want to pray for. I have burdens I want to address and people I want to bless. When it all boils down to it, I want to tell the lost, the luke-warm and any I can get to listen that there is hope in Jesus Christ!

It is those changes of heart which are the most profound and powerful changes I have experienced. It is also in the changes of the heart where the common ground of the testimonies of believers can be found. While none of us share the same exact details and experiences of our testimonies, we do share the same God dwelling within the hearts of all the regenerate.

These things have come to pass not because I went jogging and ate my Wheaties this morning. They have not come to pass because I am a nice guy or because I am so smart. They came to pass because when I had nowhere to turn but to Jesus—as I turned to Him, He delivered me. Then, when my heart began to say "Now what?" He put a Bible in my hand. I can look at all of these things which are a part of my life today and remember how different it used to be. And then I have to remember what made the difference. It was Jesus. He—The Creator[5]—is the maker of the difference.

-What He said-

"That he rent his clothes."

One of the great gifts of Scripture is that it not only reveals the truth about God, but it also reveals the truth about us. Scripture reveals what we were intended to be,[6] the occasion of sin and its influence upon us,[7] and the utter hopelessness we have in ourselves in returning to and enjoying the Lord's purpose for us.[8] It reveals the perpetual tendencies of sinful man,[9] and all his potential struggles with temptation and delusion. It is these truths about man that are so key in bringing us in desperation to the Lord.[10] A continual commitment to the pages of Scripture is one of the surest avenues to maintaining appropriate perspectives upon both our need to depend upon the Lord and the extreme peril we are in the instant we decide *not* to depend on Him. In short—The Word helps us to stay broken before Him.

The Bible is the ultimate measuring stick, the ultimate barometer, the ultimate gauge. It is the life-giving breath of God which, in all its profitability toward men, will reveal the truth about God and His grand story of redemption. The Light upon its pages will expose man's love for darkness and, as the breath of God blows conviction upon our hearts,[11] will turn us from darkness toward the available righteousness of which we stand in need. It will bring us from the darkness *"into the marvelous light."*[12] The Word will never teach us wrong, never lead us astray and always stand. If we are to live the powerful, productive life of the believer broken before the Lord, we must be broken before His Word.

"All Scripture is given by inspiration of God and is profitable for doctrine, for reproof, for correction, for instruction in righteousness." - 2 Timothy 3:16

CHAPTER 5

Broken before the Throne

**The influence of the Truth of the Word upon the
prayer life of the believer. A brief examination
of types of prayer and the responsibility to pray
Biblically. Rejoicing in the promise and experience
of receiving His answers and direction.**

*"In my distress I called upon the LORD,
and cried unto my God." - Psalm 18:6*

In yielding to Scripture as it paints an ever-clearer
portrait of our need for Him, it is inevitable that we
will develop a desire not only to continue to exercise
that need (through further dependence upon the Word),
but also to *express* that need. We're going to need to
talk to the Lord about what He has said to us. Scripture

is clear—God's people will want to talk to Him.[1] This further expression of our desperate dependence upon the Lord comes through prayer. When we receive His message through the Word, prayer is the first form of response. While eventually our response to the Word will result in action (if it doesn't, we've completely missed the point), before we move an inch we need to talk to Him about it—lest we move an inch without Him.

I have often heard "there are some things we don't need to pray about." Be careful with this one. Yes, we understand that we don't need to ask God if we should witness for Him or feed the poor. The Bible tells us so. However, we need to continually remember that we can't accomplish anything worthwhile apart from Him. So, for example, the manner and means by which we approach what the Lord has called us to do in feeding the poor need be a matter of continual inquiry before Him.

I have yet to revisit the subject of prayer and not come away feeling as if I don't do enough of it. Yet I often find that when my prayer-life is waning, it is less a matter of diligence and more a matter of perspective of which my apathy is a symptom. Note again the value of brokenness over the Word as I explain what I mean.

On a few different occasions, I have taught and preached a series on prayer. In the weeks preceding and during the particular series, I would spend time pondering the various texts dealing with the subject addressed. As the Word exposes the great value, privilege, and charge we have concerning the institution of prayer, it invariably begins to work on my heart. My time of preparation and information gathering becomes a time of prayer and repentance. The Truth in His ever-convicting and refreshing fashion will renew my perspective once again. This perspective reveals not only how much I need Him, but also reminds me of all the available help I leave laying out on the proverbial table when I don't talk to God.

The encouragement of Paul to Timothy in his proclamation of the Word comes to mind. *"Reprove, rebuke, and exhort."*[2] The Word exposes, gives us our always needed (no apologies) smack across the back of the head, and encourages us in His direction. The truth concerning prayer will drive us to our knees in dependence so that the development that the Lord intends for us might continue.

Once again, an important starting point regarding prayer is the perspective with which we approach it. Scripture tells us to *"come boldly unto the throne of grace."*[3] This boldness does not involve any irreverence or a cavalier attitude, but a recognition of the authority by which we as believers approach the throne. Prayer is the great honor and privilege of the believer. It is our access and approach to Almighty God Himself. It is by no other way than through the shed blood of Christ which poured from His torn body[4] that we have this amazing access to God. We need not a priest to approach the throne, for by the blood of Christ applied to our lives, we are priests ourselves—part of the *"royal priesthood."*[5] To hold the institution of prayer in light regard is to belittle the work of the cross. It is to trample the blood of Christ.

This perspective may challenge the "I-had-a-cup-of-coffee-and-chatted-with-my-buddy-God-this-morning" approach to prayer. It is, however, one rooted in Scripture that will promote an appropriate attitude toward our King as we open our hearts and lips in preparation to speak to Him.

-Approaching Prayer-

"In my distress"

We recall, once again, that we have acknowledged a need for desperate dependence upon Him and have committed to exercising that dependence through dependence upon the Word. As we now begin to express that dependence through the great privilege of prayer, how should we do it? Again, should our approach be to "wing it?" Just do what comes natural (a.k.a. what you feel like)? We glance here at two forms of scriptural instruction in addressing these questions. These forms of instruction are example and direction.

One tragically great example of a self-ascertained manner of approach to the throne can be found in 1 Samuel 13:9. As King Saul was under the threat of the Philistine army, in a panic he offers a sacrifice to the Lord (an accompaniment to supplication) instead of waiting for Samuel to do so. Unfortunately, Samuel and not Saul was the appropriate one to offer this supplication. Saul had all kinds of ideas he had come up with as to why it was appropriate to do what he thought was right. At a glance, his assessment might seem valid to us:

"Saul was just doing what he thought was right—right?"

"Isn't that good enough—good intentions?"

"God knows my heart doesn't He? He knows what I'm *trying* to do…"

At the end of the day, Saul had breached the directions of God, who *always* has the most valid of all assessments. The consequence for this king was great. It cost him the throne![6] While this example involves an improper sacrifice, the implications of approaching the Lord in an un-prescribed manner are clear. This doesn't mean neglecting God's directions will always cost us everything as it did Saul, but we must come to terms with the reality that to neglect the directions of the Lord is *always* costly. We must further ask ourselves the question: "How much are we willing to spend?" You see, there is no price tag on the items at the "Neglecting God's Direction" store. It is imperative that we develop a mindset as a part of our brokenness and dependence before Him that we're not going to shop at that store at all. Don't even bother to window shop because we will never know the cost until after we have swiped our credit card and signed our name to it.

Jesus purchased our pardon. He did not purchase us a license to be rebellious without consequence. If fact, if our attitude and actions dictate that we believe that He has, it would do us well to look and see if we have ever accepted Jesus' purchase for the pardon of our sin in the first place. *"What then? shall we sin because we are not under the law, but under grace? God forbid. Know ye not, that to who ye yield yourselves servants to obey, his servant ye are to who ye obey; whether of sin unto death or of obedience unto righteousness?"*[7]

Acknowledging our need for direction in execution is a great place to start with prayer. We might even feel compelled to say something like, *"Lord, teach us to pray.*"[8] The answers really are there, aren't they? (We're all down with where "there" is now, right?)

As we look to the directions of our Lord in Luke Chapter 11, we find a beautifully clear framework regarding our prayers. Never intended to be repetitive recitation (See Matthew 6), it covers the general bases of how we are to approach the throne. This approach involves specific actions and a specific attitude. While I recognize that many have broken down the primary types of prayer found here and have categorized them in various and extremely helpful ways, I still feel compelled to make brief note of the specific actions or types of prayer before we address the attitude behind it.

First, we find in our Lord's example of prayer a priority in ascribing worth to God. Grateful praise is acknowledging all that the Lord is. The more time we spend broken before the Word, the more meaningful this action of prayer will become. A high regard for Scripture will subsequently result in a reverence for the name of God. The Word teaches us that His name is "hallowed." As we reverence His name, we will see more and more the implications of His name (The Lord our: Supply, Healer, Banner, Peace, etc.) as set forth in Scripture upon our lives. A worshipful heart is a heart that continually grows in the knowledge of who God is *and* His influence upon us through His grace. A heart that is not grateful before the throne will see no need to depend upon the throne for grace.

Second, there are the supplication prayers. This is the acknowledgment of our continual *need* for Him. Again, this is done in light of the praise that recognizes who He already is and what He has already accomplished. In many ways, these supplications are prayers over what is yet to come. We don't know what's coming down the pike. We don't know what we're going to need tomorrow or in the next moments, but what we do know is that we'll need Him then as much as we need Him now when we get there. Our supplications can be powerful in maintaining tomorrow's brokenness before the Lord today.

Third, prayers of intercession are sprinkled throughout the prayer instruction indicating the Lord's direction for us always to have others on our minds as we come to the Lord in prayer. As we look to the text,[9] all of the aspects of the "Lord's" prayer are made with collective needs in mind (our, we, us). You know, the guy next to me needs the Lord just as much as I do. Not more, not less, the same. Regarding our subject of brokenness, beware especially of thinking that people need the Lord more than you. When we make the statement "He/She *really* needs the Lord," no matter how well-intentioned, we come dangerously close to the attitude that our assessment of said person is made from the vantage point of one who has it all together. I realize we can, in our gratitude, develop the appropriate attitude that "God's given me everything I need," but we *still* need Him. Our very breaths are in His hand.[10]

Finally, there are the prayers of confession. Those prayers that acknowledge our wrongdoing and request the reconciling forgiveness that can only come from Him.[11] I will address this need in further detail in the next chapter. It is, however, worth noting here in the spirit of maintaining a consistent brokenness before Him—as daily we need God's sustaining (daily bread), daily we need forgiveness.

As the instruction of the Lord continues through the early verses of Luke Chapter 11, there is a little hypothetical story that Christ gives to reveal another action important regarding prayer. That action is persistence. This is not because He wants us to beg. This would not be consistent with other Scripture involving the description of God's character. Many times, directions of God are given not so much as a revelation of His character, but of ours. Remember, God knows all about our "quick forgetters." So we readily receive Christ's not so subtle reminder that we can easily become neglectful in depending upon Him.

It is through these actions of prayer that our desperation for the Lord is expressed. Each type of prayer acknowledges in some way either dependence or the reason to depend upon the Lord. Neglect of these directions will come at great cost.

-Attitude and Prayer-

"I called upon the LORD."

Having reminded ourselves of the prescribed actions (or types of prayer) given by our Lord involving prayer, it is important as well to reflect upon the attitude or condition of the heart from which they are expressed. We need to remember to whom we're talking. If we're truly talking to the Lord, whose name is "hallowed," all of our prayers should then center upon one foundational desire: the accomplishment of God's will. It is, after all, all about Him and what He wants, not me and what I want, right? This will move our hearts and prayers from dictation and direction ("God, I want a pony.") to devotion and dependence (Lord, *thy will be done.*)

This is the kind of "God logic" expressed toward the end of Romans 11 which transitions into the behavioral instruction beginning in Romans 12. In light of the *"depth of the riches both of the wisdom and knowledge of God,"* we present ourselves *"living sacrifices."*[12]

It literally makes me want to scream when I overhear believers discussing their desires, even when they are the most benevolent of ones, and I hear someone say,

"Have you prayed about it? You know, the Bible says 'you have not because you ask not.' It says, 'ask and ye shall receive.'"

They'll even throw in the "ye," so the counsel sounds all Scriptural.

Note the wonderful promises found in Luke 11:9-10:

> *"And I say unto you, Ask, and it shall be given unto you; seek, and ye shall find; knock, and it shall be opened unto you. For everyone that asketh recieveth; and he that seeketh findeth; and to him that knocketh it shall be opened."*

These promises are given *after* the very specific instruction of the Lord already mentioned. They come through His applied power in the life of the believer when yielding to *His direction*. It is only when we, as believers, seek God's will for our petitions and intercessions that we can enjoy these promises. He will give us *"the desires of our hearts"* when we *"delight ourselves in him."*[13]

Attitudes that don't acknowledge the will of God as a priority when we pray are ones of which we need to be extremely wary. The instructional warnings found in James Chapter 4 make this point wonderfully clear.

Sometimes we just want things we don't have: *"Ye lust, and ye have not:"* In these times we often don't acknowledge or inquire as to the will of God. At times, we are so focused on our own desires it doesn't even *enter into our minds* to regard the Lord at all in said matter. The pursuit of self-fulfillment can lead us down roads where we will do whatever we need to do to get what we want: *"ye kill, and desire to have and cannot obtain:"* For the believer, these pursuits rarely work out and are never fulfilling—it's never what we hope it will be. This is an aspect of the sufficiency of His grace as well for He will always endeavor to show us the insufficiency of our own—the insufficiency of self-reliance. The harder we rangle and try to have our way, the more it is revealed in the ensuing calamity that we haven't relied on Him: *"ye fight and war, yet ye have not, because ye ask not."* We are losing and missing out because we haven't relied upon Him!

Eventually on this kamikaze flight of self-fulfillment it may dawn upon us that things aren't working out because the Lord is nowhere in any of it. So we start to pray: "Lord, I want a pony." And we pray *hard.*

"Lord, I want a pony, I want a pony, I want a pony, I want a pony! (Didn't the Lord say I was supposed to pray persistently? Well, I'm starting to right now, ok?) James sums up just how well all this works out in his statement: *"Ye ask, and receive not, because ye ask amiss, that ye may consume it upon your lusts."*[14]

Unfortunately, what often results in the heart and mind of the believer so misguided in this fashion is this:

"I prayed. You told me I have not because I (I mean ye) asked not. I asked and I still don't have *so you're not answering my prayer."*

The reason we feel as if our prayers are bouncing off the ceiling is because they're not directed at God at all—they arc directed at us! They're not prayers that are departures from our own will and seeking the will of God to be accomplished. This kind of praying is seeking to impose our own will upon God. No wonder we're not getting much feedback! Actually, when we're praying in this manner and we're not hearing anything, we had better be glad about it. Instead of giving us what we want, He may just give us what we deserve. (Gulp.)

It must always be remembered that the nature of prayer itself is an action of dependence upon the Lord. We depend upon Him to listen, care and respond in some way according to His will. It is appropriate to have an aspect of caution involved in our prayer that our prayers reflect the desperate condition of a people who realize they must depend on Him.

-Acceptance of our Desperate Prayer-

"And cried unto my God."

So great is our need for God's help. Scripture reminds us we don't even know *what* to pray for on our own and that our prayers are in continual peril of lacking in quality and character. Romans Chapter 8 reminds us, *"we know not what we should pray for as we ought."*[15] This text also reveals (Praise God!) that it is our Helper, God the Holy Spirit, who directs the prayers of the believer according to God's will. Yielding to His leadership ("Lord, teach me to pray"), as we are broken before him in prayer, will powerfully influence our lives with His will. This is a wonderful alternative to self-destructively seeking to impose our will upon Him.

I realize that these reflections upon prayer are in no way exhaustive. There are many excellent and practical books on the subject which have been a great instruction to me. I do, however, always want to routinely encourage believers in the direction of the greatest Book and greatest instruction there is on any subject we need to know: The words of the Word.

Through the exercising of our dependence upon the Word for instruction, more and more the expressions of that dependence through prayer will be according to His will. Psalm 102:17 promises us, *"He will regard the prayers of the destitute, and not despise their prayer."* Broken before the throne in dependence and desperation before Him, as He aligns our will with His, we will increasingly enjoy the great power of the Almighty calling the shots in our lives. It will not be a matter of suspicion if the Lord might be directing our lives, it will become a matter of fact. Standing on the promises of God involves a whole lot of kneeling.

"And this is the confidence that we have in him, that, if we ask anything according to his will, he heareth us: and if we know that he hear us, whatsoever we ask, we know that we have the petitions that we desired of him." – 1 John 5:14, 15

CHAPTER 6

Broken over Sin

**Acknowledging the severe detriment of
a light regard toward sin. Recalling the
necessity of Christ's sacrifice for sin.**

*"If we say that we have no sin, we deceive ourselves
and the truth is not in us. If we confess our sins,
He is faithful and just to forgive us our sins and to
cleanse us from all unrighteousness." – 1 John 1:8, 9*

"I'm only human." It's the great mantra of the
unrepentant believer. While we need always to recognize
the insufficiency and fallibility of our humanity, the
nature of fallen man should *never* be an excuse for the
believer. Along with "the Devil made we do it," it is
the ultimate cop-out from the aspects of responsibility

necessary to walk as believers. We know we can't fix sin on our own. So our responsibility lies solely and simply in dependence upon Him. When we belittle sin, we are depending upon ourselves as the fixer—by not fixing but offering our perspective upon sin as an excuse to overlook it. The belittling of sin is a severe tragedy among God's people. When we do, we distance ourselves from the available power over it.

How we belittle sin is an issue of attitude about it as well. Much like our attitude toward prayer, if our focus regarding sin is directed toward our will and not the Lord's, we will find ourselves continually lacking in the power department. You see, as long as sin is viewed as something that gets in the way of accomplishing personal wants, we will constantly struggle with the same sins over and over. This is because the Lord is not going to empower a self-centered lifestyle. The Lord certainly desires for us to live victoriously as believers, but that victory will always come on His terms and not ours. It will come when the intent and the attention is His glory and not ours. The early verses of Hebrews 12 remind us of an ability we will have in laying aside *"besetting"* sin when our focus is upon *"Jesus, the author and the finisher of our faith."*[1]

Acknowledging God's will for the sin in our lives is key to living powerfully for Him. He intends for us to take sin seriously and not to be mired down in its bondage.[2] It is the Word and not our personal observations that reveal the magnitude and seriousness of sin. While we may get a glimpse of sin's damage and consequences in the observation of our lives and the lives of others, it is the Word which will expose sin's consequence to our hearts: *"the law entered that offense might abound"*[3] Remember, Scripture not only reveals to us who God is but who we are as well. Before regeneration, we were sinners in need of a Savior, hopeless apart from Him. As the redeemed, we are sinners saved by grace, freed from the penalty of sin by the application of the redeeming work of the cross to our lives as we looked to Him in faith. We are, however, sinners saved by grace who *still constantly need the Savior to break continually the power of sin over our lives.*

Paul understood intimately this struggle with sin and the hopelessness we experience as believers in overcoming it: *"O wretched man that I am! Who shall deliver me from the body of this death?"*[4] Do you hear the desperation of his statement? These are the words of a *believer* broken over the sin in his life. He had previously expressed his desire, his want, to overcome his sinful nature. Finding effort and decisions toward sin to be insufficient, he comes in broken desperation to the Lord. This is always the only true hope there is. But again, if we're ever going to come running to the Lord in this desperate dependence for His intervention for the sin in our lives, we need to have the proper attitude toward sin.

The hypocrisy with which we, at times, approach this "issue" is staggering. How often do we desire to be rid of those sins that are inconvenient, destructive or cause defamation and regard other sins without these immediate effects as quietly acceptable? Isn't this less a brokenness over sin and more a burden for our own comforts? How often are we enraged over the progressively "sinful society" in which we live (you know, when I was a kid...), but fail to acknowledge that the society is what it is because *we have failed as believers to influence it?* Solomon had something to say on this: *"Say not thou what is the cause that the former days were better than these? For thou dost not inquire wisely concerning this."*[5]

Are we willing to consider that we're really not too burdened over the sin in our own lives at all or not nearly as much as we like to think that we are? Do we realize how powerfully (and detrimentally) influential this form of apathy regarding sin is upon the people we are around—both the lost we are to be evangelizing and the regenerate we are to be discipling?

I'm expressing these thoughts in this direct manner because by now you're either on board with this hard look at ourselves or this book is holding up the short leg of the couch. With every examination of scriptural truth, we should be brought further and further down the desperate road of dependence. This is a road where we arrive at the destination of "no other option" but throwing ourselves down before Him and saying, "Lord, please forgive me. Lord, please deliver me."

Sin is a really big deal. A really, really big deal. Any sin. All sin. My words will never express the magnitude of the situation of sin adequately. His will.

"Father, if thou be willing, remove this cup from me: never the less not my will, but thine be done." (Luke 22:42)

"Father, forgive them; for they know not what they do" (Luke 23:34)

"For he hath made him to be sin for us, who knew no sin; that we might be made the righteousness of God in him." (2 Corinthians 5:21)

"But he was wounded for our transgressions, he was bruised for our iniquities: the chastisement of our peace was upon him; and with his stripes we are healed." (Isaiah 53:5)

"But God, who is rich in mercy, for his great love wherewith he loved us, even when we were dead in sins,

hath quickened us together with Christ, (by grace ye are saved)." (Ephesians 2:4, 5)

Jesus took sin seriously. It is such a big deal, He came and died to pay for it. Not for His sin, but for ours. *"And ye know that he was manifested to take away our sins; and in him is no sin."*[6] Sin nailed Him to the cross.

One Sunday, about a year into my walk with the Lord, I was in Sunday school listening to the teacher teach on the Passion. As he described the torture and agony of the scourging and the crucifixion, I remember writing a little note in the margin of my Bible. I thought I was being all deep and philosophical as I wrote, "What was on the mind of the men holding the whip and the hammer as the Lord suffered and died?" A year or so later I came across that note once again and had to just hang my head as I thought of my own sin that had driven in the nails.

Now we're ready to talk about sin.

Do you see the pattern emerging? If we're going to be desperate and broken before the Lord today, we need to go back to the cross to remember what desperate is. If we're going to be broken before the Word today, we need to go back to the cross to remember what Truth is. If we're going to be broken before the throne today, we need to go back to the cross to remember why our prayers can be heard and what He endured to accomplish the privilege. If we're going to be broken over sin, we must return to the cross and remember what nailed Jesus to it.

Without a view of the cross fixed in the sight and heart of the believer, distractions will overwhelm and ensnare, motivations will wane, and sin will not be a big deal at all.

-I still sin-

"If we say that we have no sin."

So, we must raise the matter of being willing to admit that sin is a problem in our lives. No problems, no solutions, no progress, right? No questions, no answers, right?

"We're not finished products,"[7] It is one of the easiest things to say and one of the hardest things to live. If we say it, and there are no changes or maturing in the life from which the words came, then the words are just an excuse to sin. When it is a statement of humble admission, it will come from a life that is depending on the Word for reproof and direction and is continually confessing transgression before the throne. It is here where we will experience the power of the resurrected Lord cleansing and developing our lives. The maturing life of the believer is not only about what is added to the life but is in what is taken away as well. We must maintain the attitude that there is always something that needs to be gotten rid of (sin) and that it is a really big deal (and again we look to the cross to see why).

Paul's exhortation to the church in Ephesians 4:22 regarding the maturing of the believer is, *"that ye put off concerning the former conversation the old man, which is corrupt according to the deceitful lusts."* Here we see a particular emphasis upon the severity of sin. It will ruin us—render us useless! If sin is still running rampant in the life of the believer, it will be a constant impediment to growth, hence the emphatic tone of the text. It will keep us from living *"unto the measure of the stature of the fullness of Christ."*

So it is necessary that we come to the place where we maintain a willingness to admit we sin. It is necessary that we come to the place where we recognize that sin is a big deal and that it needs to be removed if we are to move away from immaturity. But how do we identify the sins that cause such struggle in our lives? Some are readily identifiable and obvious to us. Some are not. Do we just try to figure it out on our own? (Sound familiar?) Do we go just based on our feeling—if we feel bad about it, *then* we've sinned? (Watch out!)

While Scripture calls us repeatedly to self-examination, this too is nothing that we can accomplish on our own. *"O LORD, I know that the way of man is not in himself,"*[8] said Jeremiah. On our own we're *always* going to have views that are subject to being distorted and biased.

David recognized his inadequacy in identifying his own transgressions. He was willing to look and to accept what was found, but he needed the Lord's help in doing it.

"Search me, O God, and know my heart: try me; and know my thoughts: and see if there be any wicked way in me, and lead me in the way everlasting." (Psalm 139:23, 24)

In Chapter One of this text I mentioned a little inventory-type exercise using the Word which helped me to remember the desperation of the day I met Christ. Well, the Bible is a book that is *full* of useful inventories. It is constantly God's message to us. Using the message of God is how we prepare ourselves for God's response to the prayer of David (Psalm 139 above) when we pray it. We pray, we hold our lives up to the Word and the Word exposes the dark corners (or rooms) in our lives. This is *specifically* done as we look at the various identifications in Scripture of the things we are to be doing that we don't, and the things which we are doing which we should not be (sin). That's pretty simple.

As our sin is exposed through this prayerful, pondering process, we confess and are cleansed, and have the Word already open before us to *"instruct us in righteousness."* This is the continued action of repentance in the life of the believer: The action of turning from sin and turning to Him. The Word exposes the sin, and the Word prescribes the righteous "replacement action" to which we are to yield ourselves. The manner, if you will, that we are to turn to Him. The Word will remove the mystery of, "I've identified my sin and confessed it, now what do I do?"

So, let's say we're pondering away in our daily time in the Word. As we meditate upon the Word, we are pausing to pray—praising God for His provision of Truth and asking for the accomplishment of His will in Truth's application to our lives and the lives of the brethren. As we pray, the Spirit makes intercession for us guiding both our prayers and pondering in the direction of the subject of mean things I've said recently. The harsh words said to, perhaps, a family member come to heart. Because we are growing in the familiarity of the Word, Ephesians 4:29 comes to heart as well. *"Let no corrupt communication proceed out of your mouth."* Well, it has, and the Word has exposed our sin and the Spirit has convicted us as well. Having acknowledged our wrong-doing, we come to the throne with this admission and ask for forgiveness. Restored in our fellowship with Him, we then are nigh unto the power which enables us to turn to better things—to righteous things. To use our mouths for their godly purpose of "edifying" and "ministering grace to the hearers." It's really pretty cool how He does this. Another movement in the sovereign symphony of the Lord.

Unfortunately, for so many of us believers, repentance was an event that took place at the time of re-birth and nothing more. Repentance in this view is a "one-time thing." Boy do we miss out when we have this perspective! Nothing could be further from the truth. Repentance is not an event, it is a *lifestyle*. This lifestyle is the difference between, "I've turned to God, and I'm done." and, "I'm never as close to the Lord as I could be." We can see first-hand these attitudes as they are played out in our lives.

The first attitude manifests itself in all the immaturity, dissatisfaction and self-centeredness of spiritual infancy. It breeds inward-looking churches whose greatest concerns are their own enjoyments and comforts. It creates an environment of exclusivity where phrases like, "We like our little church," and, "That's not how we do things around here," are practically written into the by-laws. I have gotten a lot of hard looks when I've used the words "Church-club." I guess the first rule about Church-club is that you don't talk about Church-club. (I'm not pointing a finger. I'm part of the body of Christ and I am responsible too.)

The second attitude can be seen in and described with one word: Humility. Where we are grateful and glorify God for what He has accomplished and allowed into our lives, and we realize that He's not finished yet. It shouldn't be discouraging as we examine ourselves in the reproving rays of the Word. It should be exciting! This is because as he cleanses and matures us through this process of examination, a question will begin to emerge in light of the transformation which is taking place in us: Just how far will He bring us? Just how far will he allow us to go? Well, all the way to Glory!

"Beloved, now are we the sons of God, and it doth not yet appear what we shall be: but we know that, when he shall appear, we shall be like him; for we shall see him as he is. And every man that hath this hope in him purifieth himself even as he is pure." (1 John 3:2,3)

That's the kind of stuff that should make us want to get out of bed in the morning. It's one of the ways we *live* like we're one step closer to Glory today.

-Denial and Delusion-

"We deceive ourselves and the truth is not in us."

Do we struggle to admit that we sin? Admitting to mistakes is not easy. We really need to check ourselves on this. When a wrong-doing has been identified by ourselves or even others, how often are the first things which come to mouth or mind an excuse or some kind of defense? ("Yeah but…I'm only human.") The Scripture mentioned above illustrates for us the kind of statements made by the life of one unwilling to admit their sin. It's pretty rough stuff.

In the first place, when we don't admit that we have sin in our lives we are just flat out lying to ourselves. This form of self-delusion is so crippling simply because pride always is. Remember in Daniel when King Nebuchadnezzar was warned by his dream to *"break off thy sins by righteousness."*[9] His pride ignored the true warning of God. His delusion brought him to a place where he was walking in the palace contemplating the greatness of his own self, and that his own greatness had caused the rise of Babylon! This is the same guy identified as *"my servant"*[10] by the Lord. It was the Lord which gave him the kingdom yet his prideful delusion determined otherwise, and he would not admit he had sins to "break off." Scripture tells us the same hour he was struck crazy and out in the field eating grass with the animals.[11]

I don't want to eat grass. I'm sure it tastes terrible.

Unwillingness to admit sin also makes the statement that the Word of God has not influenced our lives. Here we step foot on a very troubling road of contemplation. The Truth not *"in us"* can certainly mean that we have refused to grow in the knowledge and application of the Word. It can mean that we have decided to leave aside the one weapon we have to enter the fray with as believers, to lay aside the lamp and light that is to guide us on our journey, to disregard the answer key to every test and trial we will face. What a waste indeed.

The most horrible statement of all, however, which we potentially make when we refuse to admit sin or attempt to disregard and belittle sin, is that the Truth has not delivered us *at all*. That we don't know Jesus as our Savior. That we have not been touched by His redeeming grace. That we, in desperation, have never come to Him in brokenness over our sin—sin over which we were convicted that separates us from Him and which put Him on the cross. This refusal to admit sin makes a statement that sin is not a big deal to us today because it has *never* been a big deal. If you've never been desperately broken over sin and its influence, if you've spent years trying to catch a wave of motivation to "live for Jesus" without having stepped into the ocean of His grace—now's the time.

He made a way. He made a way for us to have victory over the sin that so shackles us. That way was the payment made at the cross. He went by way of the cross to pave the road of redemption and freedom for us all.

-Continual Confession-

"If we confess our sins, he is faithful and just to forgive us our sins, and to cleanse us from all unrighteousness."

The Words of 1 John 1:9 are written to the body of Christ to restore the broken fellowship of the believer with the Lord caused by sin. The beautiful promise of these words is the privilege of every believer. They are prayed from the heart that is willing to admit that perpetually we are guilty of sin and are always in desperate need of Him. This attitude of admission and constant willingness to repent will yield a maturity and strength as we draw ever closer to our advocate—*"Jesus Christ the righteous."*[12]

I *still* need Him. I *still* need His forgiveness... Because I'm the biggest schmuck you'll ever meet. I'd take this kind of desperate brokenness before Him over "look at all I've become" any day.

Paul used the present tense speaking of his own sin as he encouraged Timothy to accept the truth that:

"This is a faithful saying, and worthy of all acceptation, that Christ Jesus came into the world to save sinners; of whom I am chief." – 1 Timothy 1:15

CHAPTER 7

Sincerely Broken

The necessity of sincerity and the heart behind the Christian walk. Evaluating the motivation of believers regarding Christian activity. Acknowledging the need and value of humility.

"And whatsoever ye do, do it heartily, as unto the Lord, and not unto men." – Colossians 3:23

"Do it. You'll get a blessing out of it."

"Tithe. God said He'd pour out a blessing on you."[1]

"Hey man, what you give up today, God said you'd get it back 100 times!"[2]

I am continually amazed at what motivates us as believers. For people who have been impacted by the selfless love of Jesus Christ, we often find ourselves using some pretty selfish motivation to reciprocate that love. There is no question that God makes wonderful promises to His obedient followers. But is it right to use the potential receiving of those promises as a primary means of motivation for our demonstrations of obedience? When we obey in this fashion aren't we more interested in what we get out of it then in what is being accomplished and expressed through it?

"Christian Mercenary" is an expression I have used to describe the actions of true believers who have recognized the sovereign superiority of God, but who fail to see that He is not just simply the highest bidder for our allegiance. He's not to be the "best bet" or the "biggest payoff." He is all of these things but that is not to be our perspective, for when it is, our relationship with Christ becomes or remains all about *us*. It's supposed to be all about Him, isn't it? Like so many of these perspectives, we rarely say these kinds of things out loud, but often our mannerisms and approaches to obedience scream them.

Our relationship with the Lord is, in many ways, established because we have hope in getting something out of it. However, it is the grossest of immaturities when our walks don't grow from that attitude. Yes, I receive from Jesus today and am much more aware of all He does for me now than I was the day I was reborn. But while our relationship with Jesus Christ begins with receiving, it will grow as we grow into *responding* with what we have received.

Earlier, in Chapter Three, I mentioned that we are all a bit deluded about the quality of our Christian walk in some way. The sincerity with which we approach the exercises and expressions of our faith is essential in our walk as believers broken before Him. The more willing we are to recall and accept our continual desperate need for Him, the more our pondering on the Word and prayer will be dependently founded. Lack of sincerity and going "through the motions" of Christianity should be enormous red flags for us. Do we ever struggle with motivation to be obedient to the broken exercises and expressions already mentioned in this book? I'm sure to most all of us, the facts that we are to remember what God has done for us, spend time in His Word and pray are not new biblical information. Why do we so often struggle to stay motivated to do these things?

This is why brokenness is so important. As soon as we stray from the foot of the cross, as soon as we stray from that complete need for Him, the sincerity in our broken exercises and expressions begins to dissipate. We can go through all the other broken-type exercises and expressions we want but when sincerity in them is absent, when they are not truly dependent upon Him, the power we can potentially realize through them will be absent as well. And this is where we so frequently find ourselves: living uninspired and un-empowered lives—dragging ourselves through Christian obligation rather than joyfully surrendering to Christian obedience. Man, do we miss out when this is how it is!

You see, when our obedience is not sincere, when it is not from the heart, when obedience's goal is personal reward, we completely miss the promised blessing that is supposed to come with it. We find ourselves (albeit quietly) asking that question "I've done what I'm supposed to do, Lord! Why is it not satisfying?" It is in these questions where we find the need for a continual sincerity in our brokenness. It is *so easy* to slip back into attempting achievement of a works-based deliverance in every season of our walk. The struggles of Israel in Scripture remind us of this again and again. Repeatedly,[3] the Lord makes note of the uselessness of insincere religious motion whose motivation is selfish and which tries to earn answer and attention from Him.

-All about Him-

"And whatsoever ye do."

From C.S. Lewis to Tony Dungy there are many who have described the consistency associated with integrity. Coach Dungy said it this way: "Integrity is what you do when no one is watching; it's doing the right thing all the time, even when it may work to your disadvantage." David describes the one who fears the Lord as *"he that sweareth to his own hurt, and changeth not."*[4]

As believers, we are constantly in the danger of the hypocrisy of a kind of compartmentalization of our lives. This is (as we have probably been reminded of many times before), when we are a different person on Sunday than we are on Monday. When we are different people at work than we are at the gym. We hear this in sermons and Bible study and are challenged ("I challenge you...") to be more transparent and more consistent. Have we ever stopped to ask ourselves *why* we can potentially find ourselves in this kind of hypocrisy?

Really, it's a form of a lack of faith. It's living like we don't believe that God really sees everything. Like we don't believe He cares what is seen in us. Like we don't believe in the possibility that He will both enable and inspire us to where we are doing what He would have us because we *want* to.

The grace and blessing of this kind of abandon to obedience is spoken of by Paul in his letter to the Philippians. In reflecting upon the perfect and powerful example of Christ's obedience to the Father in the previous verses, Paul offers wonderful assurance as we fearfully yield to the Lord in recognition of who He is and our own inadequacies. *"For it is God which worketh in you both to will and to do of his good pleasure."*[5] Ultimately, this power to "will and do" is available to the believer not who works himself there, but who is desperately depending upon the Lord to bring him there. And what freedom this is! No more forcing ourselves to be good Christians. No more pulling "my time" in service. "I've been doing *such and such* for *this many* years for the Lord." (We do a lot of "counting" in the church: Members, Sunday school, service attendance, years in service, etc. I wonder how healthy that really is…)

Come to think of it, insincerity of this nature was probably one of the least appealing aspects of some of the Christian "witnesses" I encountered as a lost person. I encountered so many (I know well intentioned) believers who were not joyful and peaceful but who were angry, bitter, and hyper-critical of everything going on around them. At times, I would encounter them in "evangelistic" settings where the compassion and smiles came out but the compartmentalization of their lives had already testified to me as to their sincerity. Last I checked, that's called hypocrisy. We try to laugh this off and make jokes to lost individuals who are witnesses to this kind of behavior in us:

"I don't want to be up there at that church with all those hypocrites."

"Well, there's always room for one more."

Ha. Ha.

Sadly, there are few (if any) responses to that kind of insincere witness because who wants to share in beliefs with those who obviously don't believe in what they say they do? It's tragic how difficult it is for us (absolutely me too) to see that the only way we can sincerely convince people of the difference Christ has made in our lives is when we are sincere.

It will tremendously help our sincerity when we realize that what affects one area of our lives affects our *whole* lives. That my relationship with my wife will affect the kind of relationships I have with the people at work. That my care for someone in need of help when no one is watching will affect how I help people when I'm out with a team from the church. It's not a matter of trying harder to be sincere, it's a matter of getting our hearts right before the Lord. Exposed insincerity in the life of the believer (which is the point here) is convicting, and conviction demands a response.

It's hard to show much compassion on "out-reach Saturday" when I just drove past 20 homeless people on

Tuesday and didn't give it a second thought. It's hard to be the one called upon to pray in the service on Sunday when it's the first time one has prayed since the last time they were called on to pray. While I've said (twice now) that we're all a bit deluded about the quality of our Christian walk in some way, this is *not an excuse* for insincerity. Admission of this is a call to brokenness—a call to recognize that my lack of sincerity is not a viable platform for the ability and drive to operate as a believer. What then can we do? Well, the only thing that can wash away this crippling sin of insincerity is (you guessed it) nothing but the blood of Jesus. I can't change how I think, but He can *"transform by the renewing of [my] mind."*[6] I can't change my heart but He can take my cold one and give me a *"heart of flesh."*[7] If insincerity is a form of a lack of faith may we pray in desperation and brokenness like the father of Mark 9, *"help thou my unbelief."*[8]

I write this not as one claiming victory over insincerity but as one who, through his struggles, has gotten a glimpse of sincerity's importance. When attempting to diagnose apathy in our hearts and within the body of Christ, the sincerity test is a worthwhile test to run. The questions are hard but straight forward. Am I doing what I'm supposed to be doing because it's what I want to do? Am I doing what I'm supposed to be doing for God's glory or my "blessing?"

As we are willing to ask the tough questions and face the challenges of admission and humility once again, we find (joyfully, Rom 8:28) that these are the grounds of Christian development. Specifically, here we see the development of our genuine desire to do what we know we're supposed to. It's so awesome how this works and here's how.

We've already stated the detriment of insincerity and that the struggle with sincerity is a form of a lack of faith. In a willingness to face our potential insincerity, we are facing a challenge that, like any other, we cannot face apart from Him. As we depend upon His Word to expose our insincerity and express our desperate need for forgiveness for it prayerfully, He is consequentially present in the process. Where His presence is, so is His power and we endure the examination process not through our strength but His. As we experience His power to endure the examination process, we are reminded again of the value of dependence upon the Lord. The more we see the value of depending upon Him, the more we will want to do what He wants us to do. So, we depend on Him with increased frequency. On the basis of this building faith, more and more we will have hope in the productivity of dependence upon

Him which produces sincerity in that dependence. We really *want* to depend on Him and have *faith* that His wants are what's best for us. *"Tribulation, worketh patience; and patience experience; and experience hope."*[9] The hope now, however, will have grown from the hope to receive into a hope to utilize what we have received—because that is what He ultimately wants us to do! (There will be further discussion of the action of the broken believer in the closing chapters.)

I have heard it said "You need to align your will with God's." Well buddy, I can't make myself *want or will* to do anything. I can't suddenly make myself desire what I do not desire. My only hope is to depend upon Him to change my wants. As our sincerity grows, our sincere exercises and expressions of dependence upon Him will have His power behind them.

-Whole-Hearted Humility-

"Do it heartily."

So what lies in our potential is to utilize this power with everything we have—with our whole heart. Humility is a huge aspect of this kind of "whole-heartedness." God's power without humility will not be power utilized, it will be power wielded. I'm going to assume we're down the broken road far enough that there will not be too many foolish attempts to realize His power and then utilize it for personal desire. His power will dissipate from our lives much faster than we would be able to wield it, so humility is essential. *"God resisteth the proud and giveth grace to the humble."*[10]

The life of the believer broken before the Lord will have many qualities of humility. A willingness toward self-examination, exercising dependence upon Him through dependence upon the Word and expressing dependence upon Him through prayer will be aspects of a humble believer's walk with the Lord. There are, however, a few more aspects of humility that I find necessary to address as we prepare to utilize the presence of His power in the life of the broken believer.

Humility is a necessity before other believers. If we are truly on this walk of broken desperation before the Lord, we will perpetually see that there are plenty of things we need to acknowledge, confess and repent. As we encounter believers who are as we, and the *"mote"*[11] jumps from their eye into ours, the humble perspective that acknowledges our perpetual state will be a platform for His power into our approach. Whether the occasion calls for simple encouragement and invitation in a different direction ("Hey, instead of doing *that* let's do *this* together"), or a more direct presentation of *"truth in love,"*[12] humility will greatly increase our effectiveness in their potential restoration and edification. This will be because it is obvious we are believers broken before the Lord. Nothing will so encourage someone to examine themselves than *our own* willingness to examine ourselves. It promotes the appropriate "we're all in this thing together" mentality.

Galatians Chapter 6:1 gives wonderful instruction in walking with this kind of interactive-humility. *"Brethren, if a man be overtaken in a fault, ye which are spiritual, restore such a one in the spirit of meekness; considering thyself, lest thou also be tempted."*

Also, beware of always positioning yourself as the "helper." Be sure to place yourself in the spot of "helpee" as well. No matter how seasoned or successful (blessed), the broken believer will acknowledge their constant need for help. If we were to think that we were always the ones in the position of "spiritual" and advisor, this would be prideful. So the nod here is a regard to the value of seeking counsel. The safety of a *"multitude of counselors"*[13] cannot be overstated. In the midst of this counsel seeking, it is important that we are wary not to shop for answers as Rehoboam did in 1 Kings 12. This is where we seek advice from multiple people until someone tells us what we want to hear. As broken believers before the throne, our examinations of sincerity will be very valuable in assessing the potential for this.

Some time ago, a believer shared a very practical view on the value of talking to other believers for scriptural perspectives, thoughts and assessment of decisions that I faced. Knowing that I was appropriately seeking to lean on the Word and going to the Lord in prayer he told me, "It's a good idea to bring someone else into the conversation because if it's just me and God, sometimes His voice will begin to sound a lot like mine." This is simply an acknowledgment of the fact that we will not have perfect discernment as to His will at all times. So we need other people's help. And that's cool because that's why He put them there. The humble believer acknowledges this truth of Scripture. We are built to both need and utilize what the believers around us have to offer.[14]

Humility before a believer who is also seeking a closer walk with the Lord is one of the greatest manners of exhortation we have in our Christian equipping. In this way, we participate in that person's privilege of being used of God. When we receptively (not blindly) sit down with another believer in this kind of fellowship (the main ingredient of Christian fellowship is *not* fried chicken or chocolate cake), we are giving opportunity to do what the Lord would have them do. This is a display of camaraderie which will *"stir up the gift of God which is in"*[15] them. I have seen the most seasoned of servants and ministers light up like little kids when these kinds of opportunities are before them.

The humble approach to interaction will also decrease the chance of strained relationships with each other. It is often the great diffuser of conflict. It really is ok not to have our thoughts be on the floor for every discussion, and it's ok not to be the most important one in the room with the most to say. We can often express with humility what the loudest voices of opinion cannot. This doesn't mean that we don't have worthwhile things to say. As we trust that He *"giveth grace to the humble,"* and enjoy that grace with sincere humility, His present power will guide us to the words that truly edify. After all, what He wants is for our words to *"minister grace to the hearers."*

-Powerful Sincerity-

"As unto the Lord and not unto men."

There is great power backing the believer who is sincerely broken before the Lord. Sincerity indicates that something very important has been learned not only intellectually but practically. That "something" is that the Lord's way really is the best way. Any deviations from sincere exercises and expressions of dependence upon the Lord are indications of an absent or declining faith. As mentioned earlier, this should be a grave warning to any believer to which this has been exposed.

There is such freedom in the life of the believer who sees the need to be continually sold out to Him. You see, before we can be sold out *for* Him, we need to be sold out *to* Him. Before there will be lasting qualities of diligence and faithfulness—of standing under fire, fortitude and integrity—we have to be convinced that there is no other way.

If you've even picked up a book like this, you've probably been convinced of this already. Being convinced, we examine, we read (the Bible), we pray and we observe. And when we find ourselves interacting with others motivated by what we will get out of them or to appease them so they'll go away—when we find ourselves interacting with God for (ouch) similar reasons, it's time to return to the cross. It's time to look back over our shoulders and remember the sincerity with which we said "Lord, save me!" There was a great power behind the sincerity of that brokenness wasn't there? It was a power that sincerely loved *"with an everlasting love."*[16] A power that drew with "loving kindness." A power that said "I love you" with the work on the cross and which meant every word.

> *"Grace be with all them that love our Lord Jesus Christ in sincerity. Amen." - Ephesians 6:24*

CHAPTER 8

Heart Broken

Acknowledging the importance of godly interaction within the Body of Christ. Regarding the impact interaction within the Body of Christ has upon the Church's witness in the world.

"For the perfecting of the saints, for the work of the ministry, for the edifying of the body of Christ."- Ephesians 4:12

So what's the point? Why all the surrendering and admission and petition? Why all the hard looks at one's self and inventorying? Why all the washing and equipping with the Word? Well, people need help. I'll tell you how I figured this out. It's because *I* need help.

So I take this need to the Lord, and He helps me. Broken before Him (in all the ways described and more) His power delivers and begins to produce great transformative results in our lives. We trust that this will continue as we continue to return in desperation to Him. *"Who delivered us from so great a death, and doth deliver: in whom we trust that he will yet deliver us."*[1]

Well, now what? Do we just sit and be happy? We won't stay happy for long. The sure-fire way to undo what the Lord has been doing in our development is to stop allowing Him to do it—to have an attitude that says "I'm developed enough." The danger is that if we just sit and have no other concern but for our own well-being and satisfaction we have too much time to look around and see who's getting in the way of it. If our only concern is my relationship with the Lord and what I'm getting out of it (as we mentioned in the previous chapter), we will seek to preserve it at any cost—even if our brothers and sisters are casualties of the endeavor. As our eye wanders from the cross in this fashion, our heart will follow[2] and the heart that so confidently knew the sufficiency of His grace will become unsatisfied because it is focused on the insufficiencies in others. This is a tremendous reversion back to the behavior of one who *"says in his heart that there is no God."*[3]

The dissatisfaction, grumbling, murmuring and high levels of criticism we find on occasion in our midst and in our own hearts, are symptoms of this form of arrested Christian development. We'll abuse terms like "righteous indignation" to justify our critical, combative behavior and find ourselves making moral concessions to "fix" things around us which we deem wrong. This is the climate of heart where clandestine meetings to rally support for our agendas and the unfortunate politicking amongst believers begins to set in and fester. The harder we try to apply these forms of worldliness to our operation within the Church the less happy we become. Continually, our dissatisfaction will look for something to devour, and our brothers and sisters in Christ will look like a steaming chicken leg sitting in the pew next to us.[4]

This does not mean in any way that we are not to practice Church discipline and seek to *"set in order the things that are wanting."*[5] But when these pursuits are executed from the platform of dissatisfaction and criticism (with the previously mentioned unhealthy dose of self-will), the restoring and reconciling spirit will be noticeably absent. What ends up happening is that the only way we can remove "problems" with these mindsets is by removing *people*. Is that what we're here for? To run people off?

As I have shared earlier, I have been blessed with the counsel of many fine, experienced and educated pastors. I have further been privileged with the fatherly and motherly[6] love of other great leaders in the Body of Christ. As a brand-new young minister, I had many well-meaning people around me ready to share their thoughts, experiences and advice. I am sincerely grateful for all of their efforts and continue to be so today for those who have had a continued interest in my development.

There are many great nuggets of wisdom that have been shared with me over the years, but there is one which I can recall that has been sadly universal in the advisement from these experienced Church people. Every single one has either said directly or clearly implied that I would need to develop a really thick skin because of the words and situations I would encounter as a minister. They didn't say this because of the opposition to the Gospel I would encounter on the streets. They didn't say this because of the difficulty I would have trying to minister to addicts, the homeless or the hungry. They said this because of what I would encounter from my own brothers and sisters in Christ. At the risk of sounding preachy, I will *not* be afraid to say that this should not be. Church, we should be having more important conversations with the next generation of God's called than to have to warn them about how poorly we treat each other.

After all He's done for us and invested in us, all the provision and cultivation and care—why are we so prone to lapse into these obviously destructive behaviors? Just sitting and being happy with what God has done for us is *not* the ultimate purpose in why He has done what He has done for us. We're not done yet! The true value of His regenerating, refining presence and power which we enjoy broken before the throne is *so we can do something with it! "For we are his workmanship, created in Christ Jesus unto good works, which God hath before ordained that we should walk in them."*[7] I understand that this (like most everything else I've written), is not new information. But remember, we have quick forgetters. (That's why I'm writing it.) So we go back to the throne, we open His Word, and the warnings of Scripture are ever there to remind us of how much we need Him and all He's done for us... *And why!*

We are here to glorify Him.[8] He's blessed us to shine for Him. He saved us and is transforming us that we might testify of Him[9]—that we would testify of His love for the world. It is the greatest honor of our lives that we get to look someone in the eye who is barren, bewildered, empty and hopeless and tell them that there is hope. There is hope because Jesus Christ is alive. We can say confidently as those broken before the Lord that, "I *know* He is alive because of what He's doing in me."

-The Brethren-

"For the perfecting of the saints."

At the end of the day, treating each other poorly destroys our witness and testifies as to how much we really care about the lost. When we are indifferent about the destruction of our Christian witness, the implications are tragic. As has already been noted, a brokenness over sin and a willingness to acknowledge and repent of the sin in our lives is key to the powerful life of the broken believer. An indifference over sin and its effect on the people around us indicates just how burdened we are to live according to our ultimate purpose. Furthermore, when our sinful behavior is directed toward other believers we alienate the *very people we need* to execute our function as believers.[10] When we walk away from the power and purpose of our deliverance, the necessary partnerships we have with other believers will grow unnecessary in our eyes. People will become less and less "necessary" because we're really not doing anything but trying to satisfy our own wants once again. Eventually, we will be viewed as interferences and hindrances to one another and carnality ensues.

The "report" or reputation of the Church is as much linked to what we do as it is linked to how we treat each other. *"By this shall all men know that ye are my disciples, if ye have love one to another."*[11] It is very much our responsibility to show the world the attractiveness of the Gospel. In the same way insincerity will declare us sadly similar to the world (Chapter 7), our bickering and squabbles will as well. But we "quick forgetters" need constantly be reminded of what really *is* attractive about the gospel. The attractiveness of the gospel doesn't lie in bowling night and fish-frys (which I love by the way). Not in bouncy houses and pizza night for the kids. Not cars and houses and "God-will-pay-your-power-bill" messages. Not in lasers, extravaganzas and "come see the show" marketing strategies. The revolutionary impact of Jesus Christ upon our lives as believers should be all the marketing the Church needs. I know sometimes it seems it's not all we need as we compete with the noisy world for the world's attention, but maybe that is part of the problem. Maybe we're playing by the world's rules and methods when we are seeking to "promote" the Gospel.

The Gospel's attractiveness lies in its power. In the power which raised Christ from the dead and the power which brought us to life when we were *"dead in [our] trespasses and sins."*[12] As supernatural power is seen working in God's people, He will be promoted. That might be a little closer to *His* marketing strategy. When we look like everyone else—that's Satan's marketing strategy: Make people think that the Church is a joke when they look at it and they see hypocrisy and a bunch of people who can't get along just like everywhere else you look in the world. We know he's lost the war but in this he wins a very important battle because so many in the world will be drawn away from, and not towards the gospel.

So this kind of unholy interaction amongst the brethren should be another of those red-flag indicators that we are wandering from the cross—that we are not broken before Him!

-The Benevolent Body-

"For the work of the ministry."

One day a couple years ago, my teenage daughter brought home a little stray kitten she found under an ice box in front of the local movie theater. As she was standing there with some friends after the movie, someone heard a little "meow" in close proximity. After investigation, the kitten was found and was found to be all alone. The kitten passed from teenager to teenager:

"I don't want it."

"My parents will kill me if I bring that home."

"Just put it back where you found it."

My mushy soft-hearted daughter couldn't bear the thought of leaving it there so here it comes a little while later being toted into the house. Cue Dad stomping into the kitchen to see what all the commotion is when my daughter gets home from the movie.

"You brought another stray cat into *my* house!" (Don't you just love those unattractive reels of our lives...)

The reaction brought an obvious tension to the following hours as I attempted to lay down the law and tell people how things were going to be.

"I don't *want* another stray cat in *my* house."

The whole while this little kitten is making the most awful racket you've ever heard. It was scared and hungry. Finally, we began to pay a bit of attention to getting the little thing settled down.

"Don't bother naming it because it won't be here for long." (Ok Dad.)

My wife began to try to give it a little soft food and some milk. It was a very young kitten and was making a terrific mess wallowing in the food.

"One of you is going to need to clean up this mess." (Ok Dad.)

After a while, we had set it down in a box and tried to let it get settled. My son, who has a deep affection for cats, hung pretty close and tried to console the kitten as he continued to mew. Eventually (after Dad calmed down a bit), by the end of the evening we were all down on the floor—all five of us—trying to pet, feed, comfort, and console this little kitten. As I write this account, I am actually watching "Pip-squeak" (the now not-so-little cat) take a nap on the couch. I'll be sure to sit on that spot with all the shed fur later when I put on a clean pair of slacks.

Thinking back to the resolution of the evening when we were all trying to take care of this needy little kitten, I can't help but be reminded of God's grace in the middle of all of it and of our call to stewardship of that grace.[13] I think of how often when new people are brought, invited or find their way into the Church the kind of challenges we potentially can create for ourselves. If we have allowed ourselves to wander from the cross and regress into self-centered immaturity, it will be most obvious in those times when we are facing the challenges of bringing new people under the evangelizing wing of the Church, and new believers under the discipling wing of the Church.

After all, that's why He left us here. He didn't leave us here to preserve the integrity of the "club." He didn't leave us here to regress into an attitude where every new person is an inconvenient threat. Where conformity and quietness are prerequisites to our compassion and care. As believers who are obedient to His plan, broken before Him and yielded to His Word our heart should be broken for the needs of those we encounter. He was broken for us.

It is absolutely part of the discipling process that we both instruct and learn how to be truly helpful to the people we encounter. That we are not enablers for poor behavior, turn a blind eye to sin, or allow people to maliciously use the Church. But we need to realize that when we encounter the lost world we will encounter sin and malice. The big question is: What kind of believers will the world encounter? Will it be believers who are most interested in preserving their own comforts and own selves? Or will it be believers desperate for Him- -who see, who understand that there is no other way but His way and that His way is to care about other people. Sincere, humble believers who can powerfully, effectively share and live both the truth and the mercy of the Word of God. Believers who are so humble as to say *"neither do I condemn you"* and so bold as to say *"go and sin no more."*[14]

Remember, we are *all* a bunch of stray cats that have been adopted into His family. I am so, so glad that when I showed up on His steps one day, broken and desperate, that He didn't say, "I don't *want* another stray cat in *my* house."

-The Point-

"For the edifying of the body of Christ."

At times, we will struggle to love each other and to love the lost. The multitude of instructions in the Word about how we are to treat and relate to people is an indicator of our expected struggle.[15] In diagnosing the cause of our poor behavior toward one another, it is important for us to consider that these kinds of behaviors indicate that we have forgotten the point of what it's all about. That malice toward one another and strife among the believers is, in a way, a betrayal of the commission and call we have from the Lord. The witness we have in the world is contingent upon our love for each other.

He hasn't just saved us. (As if that wasn't enough.) He has given our lives purpose. He has *"saved us and called us."*[16]

To go and do for Christ. The recollection of His response to our desperation is of paramount importance for both the preparation and the motivation to effectively do for Him. It is key in our response to the needs of the people around us—both the brethren and the lost and dying world. It has been said in many forms before that the greatest avenue of expressing our love for the Lord is to love other people. A struggle to love the people around us is an indication that we are struggling to love the Lord Himself. An indicator like this—Isn't it enough to break our hearts?

"Beloved if God so loved us we ought also to love one another. No man hath seen God at any time. If we love one another, God dwelleth in us and His love is perfected in us." – 1 John 4:11, 12

CHAPTER 9

Broken Hands and Broken Feet

Admission of susceptibility toward apathy. The activity and the attitude of the believer "sold-out" to the Lord.

"And I will very gladly spend and be spent for you." – 2 Corinthians 12:15a

It's worth it. The products of the Lord from a life lived broken before Him shout this truth. When we are convinced of this through the track record of God's power and presence working in our broken lives, we will be increasingly motivated to "leave it all out on the field" for Him.

As believers, we do *not* operate on blind faith. It is without question that we *"walk by faith and not by sight,"* but the faith with which we step forward is based upon the perfect and powerful God who we depend upon and whose character we know. A God who has shown us over and over again that as we come in desperate dependence to Him, He answers our call according to His will. A God who shows us that His accomplished will is the greatest care for us we will ever experience. *"O that there were such a heart in them, that they would fear me, and keep my commandments always, that it might be well with them, and with their children for ever!"*[1] This is a God who has shown us that we don't *need* to see what's over His horizon because we *know* that His love for us is *"from everlasting to everlasting."*[2]

The more we allow ourselves to experience the benefit of continued brokenness before Him, the more *"persuaded"* we will be that *nothing "shall be able to separate us from the love of God, which is in Christ Jesus our Lord."*[3] The more we exercise our brokenness through brokenness over His Word, the more we will find that the Word *"effectually worketh also in you that believe."*[4] The sad alternative is the believer who is unconvinced of the interest, presence, power and purpose of the Lord. The believer who won't walk by faith, sight or any other means. A believer with a dead faith.

-Addressing Apathy-

"And I will."

It seems easier for us to spot apathy than to diagnose its cause. For a long time, I regarded my struggles with apathy as a type of spoiled complacency. I was (and at times can still be) the picture of the obese Laodicean who was "too blessed to stress."[5] (Sorry whoever came up with the bumpersticker or T-shirt. Hey, while I have you, you wouldn't know who came up with the "God is my Co-Pilot" thing would you? Tell them sorry for me too.)

I would pridefully say things like, "I have everything I need," as if I had arrived at the place in my life that the things of this world were of no concern to me any longer. I often couldn't see past the needs of the moment I was in as I lived from spiritual pay check to pay check. Operating with a zero balance in our "maturing Christian bank account" is a breeding ground for apathy for with it goes the idea that I must (somehow) be doing enough to get by:

"I'm saved—Jesus paid it all, all to Him I owe. But I don't need to spend too much. I show up at the right places and say the right things, and I more or less mean it and more or less want to…"

I doubt many of us would say that way of living sounds very appealing when we look at it in this light. In fact, it is a way of living which greatly resembles the life of the unregenerate.[6] At the times when we are willing to acknowledge our apathetic tendencies, we'll often blame it on our society and culture, the wealth of our nation and such. But all of these things are still symptoms and not causes.

The reality is that *I don't* have everything I need. That's the problem with apathy. It occurs when *we're not needy.* Show me a believer who is not needy and I'll show you one who is unmotivated. Now, please be grateful. He said, *"In everything give thanks: for this is the will of God in Christ Jesus concerning you."*[7] But boy am I lying when I say I have everything I need.

Here's what I mean. I need guidance and direction—so much so in fact that I need the Lord to show me what I need because I can't even see what I need. (Talk about needy.) I need strength and integrity. I need wisdom and power and all those things which are Christ Jesus. I can't get there on my own (broken). So I see that I am needy (desperate), and I exercise (Word) and express (prayer) that need before Him. The closer we draw (yield) to Him, the more fortitude we will have (grace) and the less apathetic we will be (power). *"Strength and gladness are in his place."*[8]

Paul understood the wonderful balance between gratitude and neediness. He understood the difference between contentment and complacency: *"I know both how to be abased and I know how to abound: every where and in all things I am instructed both to be full and to be hungry, both to abound and to suffer need."*[9]

These are the difference-making truths which when accepted will make the difference between operating like we're around the Body of Christ or operating like we *are* the Body of Christ. No question, being around the Body of Christ can be inspirational. It makes many people, even unbelievers, want to do better and make some effort toward good things. But there is no comparison between this and being an *"instrument of [His] righteousness."* One is energized by (albeit well-intentioned) personal wants and feelings. The other is energized by the power of the living God. The difference will be either eventual apathy or the endurance, faithfulness and fortitude of sold-out believers.

Jesus illustrated this difference when He identified himself as the Good Shepherd in John Chapter 10. He was sold out to the will of the Father.

"I am the good shepherd: the good shepherd giveth his life for the sheep. But he that is a hireling, and not the shepherd, whose own the sheep are not, seeth the wolf coming, and leaveth the sheep, and fleeth: and the

wolf catcheth them and scatterth the sheep. The hireling fleeth because he is a hireling, and careth not for the sheep."- John 10:11-13.

Are we hirelings or part of the Body of the Shepherd? Will we flee when enough time goes by ("I've taken my turn."), or challenges face us ("I shouldn't have to put up with this!")? Will we acknowledge that apathy and lack of fortitude identify our lack of neediness, brokenness and desperation before Him?

-Lay it all out-

"Very gladly spend."

If we are willing to acknowledge this, there is still only one solution. We return to the cross. Desperate for His sacrifice to not be seen in any way as vain by the apathy of the redeemed, we return broken back to Him. We confess the apathy we have had regarding the development and "spending" of what He has given us. So we ask him to address our neediness according to His will…*"And this is the will of him that sent me, that every one which seeth the Son, and believeth on him, may have everlasting life."*[10] Once again, through His Word, the Lord responds—with the *answer* to apathy.

Let's go back one last time and look at the record. When we had nowhere to turn, we turned to Him and He rescued us. We've acknowledged a continual need before Him and saw how His Word provided the much-needed answers for our lives. We talk to Him as His Word increasingly reveals to us His sufficiency and our insufficiency. As growing believers, we recognize how constant our dependence needs to be upon Him to mold our attitudes and hearts into His. Through yielding to His loving, transformative process, we are blessed to be filled with "the fullness of God." And we have a big wallet full of "Son-showing" to spend!

You see, In order to spend, we have to *have something to spend* and maintaining neediness before Him is the avenue to the working capital of the Kingdom. I'm not going to tell you that you can take that to the bank because the bank has already come to you! He busted open the vault of treasure that is His grace, and He wants you to go on a spending spree! There is a "Son-showing" place for us to spend our "Son-showing" funds everywhere we go. And the more we seek the accomplishment of His will in our lives, the more He gives and gives for us to spend and spend. You see, in this fashion we tap into this unbelievable trove of treasure that is limitless.

Do you remember the four lepers at the city gate in 2 Kings Chapter 7? These poor guys didn't have a chance. They were lepers which meant they couldn't even enter into the city and had to keep their distance from everybody else. All they could do was beg from a distance toward the passing people.

Well, at the time recorded in the text, Samaria was under siege by the Syrians (Arameans, but I've got my King James open in front of me) and the city gate was closed. Nobody was passing by these lepers that they might beg. They were in a desperate situation. The lepers decided to turn themselves over to the Syrians and let the proverbial chips fall where they may. If they lived they lived and if they died, they died. The best case scenario for them was probably slavery as they went to turn themselves over to the Syrians. Then the Lord intervened. He put the sound of a great army into the ears of the Syrians, and they fled.

As the lepers entered into the camp they found more food, clothes and funds than they would have ever been able to use. They began to move all the bounty around and pile it all up for themselves. Then conviction set in. They said to each other, *"We do not do well: this day is a day of good tidings, and we hold our peace:"*[11]

The lepers were thinking of all those starving people back in the besieged city who were as desperate as they had been. But, locked up inside the city, they couldn't see the abundance of help that was just a short distance away.[12] The lepers had to tell them. They had to share the treasure they had found—And they did.

Notice what is absent. They didn't lay out a bunch of terms and conditions before they went to notify the city of the abundance that had befallen them. They didn't stop and make a bunch of request forms for them to fill out, nor did they consider how the people of the city had treated them when they were at the gate in need. They just told them about the treasure they had found.

-Sold Out-

"And be spent."

The abandon of the believer broken before the Lord is not a reckless one. While there is no limit to the "God-showing" spending we may do, there are certainly limits to our own mortality—so we need to spend wisely. Also, remember that the "proof is in the pudding." If a particular method of "God-showing" is not working or having the impact it was having five years ago, we may need to consider that we should *stop doing it!* This doesn't mean that we don't hang in there through a tough season and work our way (desperate before Him) through adversities we encounter. However, we need to be careful that we're not calling thick-headed stubbornness and pride faithfulness either. That's not much of a witness of Him is it?

The Lord gives the increase and gets the glory for it. It happens according to His will in His time. But remember, the *"much fruit"* comes as we abide in the Vine.[13] In this sense, it is much less about the method and more about the Master who should always be seen in us.

We also don't equate this wisdom in spending with being miserly. Hoarding of "Kingdom resources" of any kind (time, energy, finances, possessions), betrays the "glad tidings" that we proclaim. The glad tidings Jesus was willing to bring to us at any cost. Apathetic efforts, therefore, are both the poor spending of the resources of His Kingdom *and* the lack of utilizing the available resources. It's simply not making the most of the chance we have to "spend" for Him *which He died to give us.*

There are some numbers that only God knows exactly, but we need to be aware of their existence. The number of steps I get to take in my life. The number of breaths I will breathe. The number of words I will get to say. The number of people I will meet. These numbers all add up to the number of chances I will get to *do* something for Him. How many have we used? How many have we wasted? How many do we have left? Are we living every day like it's a chance we have to spend for Jesus? Are we living each one like it might be the last chance?

Paul has always been someone who has had aspects of His life to which I could relate—I hated Christians, and Jesus made a great change about that in my life. The Bible also records some perspectives and aspects of Paul's life which I still would really like to see develop in my life as well.

When Paul was concluding what we call his third missionary journey, he was headed for Jerusalem. He'd spent years traveling and residing in so many cities and had touched countless lives with the gospel. There were times where the Spirit led him to stand boldly and times where God's sovereign hand saw fit to hold him back from the fray. The thing is, he was always *willing*. He spent his "resources" (his "God-showing") wisely, but he was always willing to empty his wallet wherever he went. He knew the great privilege, value, and abundance of the believer's life—both the trials and suffering and the strength of the Lord to carry him through it all.

As he approached the city of Jerusalem a prophet, Agabus, warned him about his impending arrest. His response is one I pray nearly daily would be the one I would like to hear come from my lips if it were how the Lord would have me "spend."

He said, *"For I am not ready to be bound only, but also to die at Jerusalem for the name of the Lord Jesus."*[14]

His sold-out attitude for the gospel is conveyed many times in Scripture, and as Paul's last words of testimony are set before Timothy and us all, he was still able to say, *"For I am now ready to be offered, and the time of my departure is at hand. I have fought a good fight, I have finished my course, I have kept the faith:"*[15]

What power and strength is available to be used and spent to the believer who is broken and desperately sold-out for Him! I love the thought of entering the Kingdom on fumes but with the throttle still running wide open.

-Stay Broken-

"For you."

I am not all of this brokenness that I have written about, but the Word has shown me that I want to be. The Word has exposed the greatness of my deficiencies, my great need for the Savior, and a great Savior who came to fill that need. With all the mercy and grace, all the power and purpose, all guiding and all the guarding available at the foot of the cross of Calvary, it is imperative that we don't wander from it. That we don't wander back toward all the foolishness, disobedience, deception, divers lusts and pleasures, malice, envy, and hatred which characterized us when we were walking in darkness—back to all the worldliness which characterized us before we saw the *"great light"*[16] that we might receive that Light and be that light for Him. That is our simple response to His grace shown us when we come broken to Him.

I spent the largest part of my life searching for peace, freedom and power in the pursuit of the fulfillment of my own desires. The harder I searched, the more tumultuous, shackled and fragile I became. Then one day, with no other option, I came crawling to the cross of Christ. Like a boxer who had just endured fifteen rounds of pummeling from a foe that he was no match for himself, I sat in the corner of the ring with the verdict of the bout already decided. As the ref was calling me to the center of the ring to declare me the eternal loser, that Man from Galilee (you know the one) stepped in between us and said to me "just stay down." He turned around, knocked out my opponent and was declared the champion of the World.

His directions to me still ring in my ears today. I've never seen someone fight like Him. *"Ye approach this day unto battle against your enemies: let not your hearts be faint, fear not, and do not tremble, neither be ye terrified because of them; for the Lord your God is he that goeth with you, to fight for you against your enemies, to save you."*[17]

So that's what I'm going to try to do. I'm going to try to just *stay down*. To stay broken at the foot of the cross desperately depending upon Him to fight all the battles I cannot win on my own. The battles of self-destruction, self-delusion and self-will. The battles of carnality and apathy. The battles of selfishness, pride, arrogance, and all the futility that goes along with all of it. With knees on the ground and nose in the Word, sewing in His righteousness and reaping in His mercy,[18] I want to hear the final bell face down on the mat—*still* broken before Him.

"I love the LORD, because he hath heard my voice and my supplications. Because he hath inclined his ear unto me, therefore I will call upon him as long as I live. The sorrows of death compassed me, and the pains of hell gat hold upon me: I found trouble and sorrow. Then called I upon the name of the LORD; O LORD, I beseech thee, deliver my soul. Gracious is the LORD, and righteous; yea, our God is merciful. The LORD preserveth the simple: I was brought low, and he helped me." – Psalm 116:1-6

Final Thoughts

It is my heartfelt prayer that the words of this text have been challenging and edifying. As I have often told the churches that I have been so privileged to serve, these Scriptures, convictions, thoughts and words have run all over me before I ever shared them with you. If these thoughts or some of the side-bar comments have been offensive, that was certainly not my intention. While I take the Christian walk and vocation very seriously, I try never to take myself too seriously or to hold myself in any kind of esteem.

I have not been trying to write like some Church outsider who has some unique perspective on things wrong with the church. I have tried, for better or worse, to give an accurate depiction of what is on my heart. To share some biblical principles that when applied to my life and the lives of others I have observed, I have seen them powerfully affect and transform.

I am not in the advice giving business. The wisdom of the Word is greater than any kind of advice I can conjure up. I endeavor always to go to the Word and present it as accurately and plainly as is possible for me to do. I don't need to take Scripture and make it practical—it is practical all on its own. It is the desire of my heart to be true to the Word of God. I am sure I have faltered and failed in this at times. It has, however, been my desire since it all began.

The day I stood in the pulpit for the very first time, like many others have testified before me of this experience, I was scared to death. I had a thousand thoughts on my heart and at the same time I felt like I couldn't hardly even remember John 3:16. But I knew there was one thing that could not be taken away or forgotten. It was who I was in Him and what He had done for me. So on that day, He gave me one simple thought that I wrote across the top of my ridiculously large stack of notes: it was to "Be Honest." To not try to be anyone other than who I was and not try to be anywhere other than where I was. This wasn't a denial of my need for continued maturity, but a charge to do the very best and to be the most sincere I could be on that day with His help. I pray I have been honest with you.

Scripture References

Preface

1- Matt 5:27, 31, 33, 38, 43

2- Acts 17:2

3- John 17:17

Introduction

1- Luke 23:41; Isa 53:9

2- Eph 5:15

3- Eph 4:13

4- Eph 2:1

5- Matt 28:18-20

Chapter 1 - Broken

1- Hos 11:2 the plural of Baal indicates here the self-centered nature of idolatry. There were differences in the "many Baals" and in the context of Hosea as a whole, it is probable that the differences in the "many Baals" were due to self-centered desires.

2- Prov 16:18

3- 2 Cor 4:4

4- Eccl 1:13-2:10

5- Eph 5:18

6- James 1:14

7- Matt 5:44, 45

8- John 4:4-29; Luke 19:1-10; Acts 9:1-20

9- Jer 1:5; 29:11

Chapter 2 - The Power of Brokenness

1- Rom 8:28-30

2- Rom 2:4

3- Matt 7:17-18

4- 1 Pet 5:8

5- Eph 6:10

6- Jas 1:14

7- Psa 119:105

8- 1 Thss 2:13

9- John 1:14

10- 1 John 3:8

Chapter 3 - Returning to Brokenness

1- John 15:5

2- Deu 6:12; Deu 9:7; Isa 51:12, 13; 2 Kings 17:38; Judges 8:33, 34; 1 Kings 11:4-6; Neh 9:16; Psa 9:17; Job 8:11-13

3- 1 Cor 10:6

4- Exo 15:24

5- 2 Sam 11

6- Hag 1:4

7- 2 Cor 7:9, 10

8- Num 13:30; 14:6, 7

9- Acts 10:15

10- Eph 2:14

11- 1 John 1:8

12- John 3:30

13- 1 John 3:3

14- Luke 17:6

15- Luke 15:11-32

16- Eph 5:16

17- James 4:8

18- James 2:17, 18

Chapter 4 - Broken over the Word

1- 2 Tim 3:15

2- 2 Kings 22:4, 5

3- 2 Kings 22:19

4- 2 Cor 5:17-19

5- John 1:3; Col 1:16

6- Gen 1:27

7- Gen 3

8- Rom 3:10; 3:23

9- Rom 1:18-32; 2 Tim 3:1-5

10- Acts 16:29

11- John 3:8

12- 1 Pet 2:9

Chapter 5 - Broken Before the Throne

1- 1 Kings 8:28

2- 2 Tim 4:2

3- Heb 4:16

4- Heb 10:20

5- 1 Pet 2:9

6- 1 Sam 13:14

7- Rom 6:15, 16

8- Luke 11:1

9- Luke 11:2, 3

10- Dan 5:23

11- 1 John 1:9

12- Rom 11:33; 12:1

13- Psa 37:4

14- James 4:2, 3

15- Rom 8:26

Chapter 6 - Broken over Sin

1- Heb 12:1, 2

2- Rom 6 (just read the whole thing)

3- Rom 5:20

4- Rom 7:24

5- Eccl 7:10

6- 1 John 3:5

7- Phil 3:12

8- Jer 10:23

9- Dan 4:27

10- Jer 27:6

11- Dan 4:33

12- 1 John 2:1

Chapter 7 - Sincerely Broken

1- Mal 3:10

2- Mark 10:31

3- Isa 1:13-15; Isa 58:3, 4; Amos 5:21

4- Psa 15:4

5- Phil 2:13

6- Rom 12:2

7-   Ezk 36:26

8-   Mark 9:24

9-   Rom 5:3, 4

10- 1 Pet 5:5

11- Matt 7:1-5

12- Eph 4:15

13- Prov 11:14

14- Eph 4:16

15- 2 Tim 1:6

16- Jer 31:3

Chapter 8 - Heart Broken

1-   2 Cor 1:10

2-   Matt 6:22, 23

3-   Psa 14:1

4-   Gal 5:15

5-   Titus 1:5

6-   1 Tim 5:1, 2

7-   Eph 2:10

8-   Isa 43:7

9-   Psa 51:10-13

10- 1 Cor 12:21

11- John 13:35

12- Eph 2:1

13- 1 Pet 4:10

14- John 8:11

15- See Chapter 3

16- 2 Tim 1:9

Chapter 9 - Broken Hands and Broken Feet

1- Deu 5:29

2- Psa 103:17

3- Rom 8:38, 39

4- 1 Thss 2:13

5- Rev 3:14-22

6- Titus 3:3

7- 1 Thss 5:18

8- 1 Chr 16:27

9- Phil 4:12

10- John 6:40

11- 2 Kings 7:9

12- Deu 30:14

13- John 15:5

14- Acts 21:13

15- 2 Tim 4:6, 7

16- Isa 9:2

17- Deu 20:3, 4

18- Hos 10:12